TOTAL CUSTOMER GROWTH

Win and Grow Customers for Life
with ABM and ABX

Adam Turinas
with Ben Person

Design and distribution by Bublish
Published by Total Customer Growth LLC

ISBN: 978-1-64704-697-2 (eBook)
ISBN: 978-1-64704-698-9 (paperback)
ISBN: 978-1-64704-699-6 (audiobook)

To our teams, our clients, our partners and the amazing network of sales, marketing and growth professionals who inspired this book. And to our loved ones for all your support.

CONTENTS

Part 4 - Get Moving. Get Scaling.

INTRODUCTION

We are two long-time sales and marketing leaders. Both of us have been responsible for growing technology firms with no sales into multimillion-dollar companies. If you are on the hook for driving growth at your firm, we have been in your shoes, and we wrote this book for you.

Adam spent two decades in marketing across multiple industries, including working with IBM, Dell, and other B2B titans. In 2012, he and a physician founded a health care technology firm, the most challenging thing he had ever done. They had a great product, and while they were very good at increasing revenues from existing customers, acquiring new ones was especially tough for them. They grew 25 times over six years, but their investors expected a much faster win rate.

The team used traditional B2B marketing but found it to be a frustrating and wasteful way to acquire new customers.

Adam knew that their marketing worked some of the time, but they struggled to create a model where marketing was measurably contributing to the firm's growth. It was the old story of knowing that 50 percent of marketing was working, but not knowing *which* 50 percent. It was only after selling the firm that Adam learned about ABM. The light switched on, and he realized what he had missed out on by not knowing about and embracing ABM.

He started his new firm in 2020 with a mission to help companies create more predictable and scalable approaches to marketing by using account-based techniques.

Most recently, Ben led the marketing transformation in a fast-growing venture-backed enterprise technology firm where he was the head of global marketing. He did so by fully embracing account-based marketing (ABM). During his tenure, the firm grew 500-fold over seven years. It was rewarding but very difficult to get that level of growth so quickly.

"The move to ABM became a no-brainer when the data proved the value in such a short amount of time. When we saw the direct correlation from intent to pipeline creation over the course of just a couple of months, we knew we were onto something that we could scale up across sales development representatives (SDRs), sales, and customer success," said Ben.

We believe that ABM is fundamentally changing the way B2B companies market. It has the potential to have the same impact on B2B marketing that Uber has had on taking a taxi and Airbnb has made on where you stay when you travel.

ABM has been around for a decade or so, but we are still early in the adoption curve. And as we will review later, those who have made the transition are seeing very positive benefits.

Adoption is starting to accelerate.

The good news is that if you are early in your journey, you are not alone. Most firms have not embraced it yet, so you can still benefit from the competitive advantages that ABM will give you, but you need to begin quickly.

ABM is evolving. For most businesses, ABM is a more effective way to acquire customers. But that is only part of the story. The principles of ABM can be applied to the whole customer life cycle to make your customer relationships more profitable and more successful over longer periods.

In our work, we speak with dozens of sales and marketing leaders every year. One of the issues that comes up most often is account-based marketing . In particular, we keep hearing these questions:

- I want to do ABM, but how do I get started?
- How do we keep and grow our current customers?
- How do we win and grow a more profitable customer base?
- How do we convince our executive team that marketing can create a competitive advantage?

Sound familiar?

If these questions are rolling around your head, this book is for you. We wrote it to help you answer these questions and develop a plan to become ABM rock stars and maybe something even bigger.

In this book, we want to achieve two goals: answer your questions about ABM and propose a new, more holistic model for making your sales and marketing more effective.

ABM is part of the answer and has emerged as *the* way to acquire new and more profitable customers.

In its simplest form, ABM can be a more effective tactic to generate demand. Over the longer term, it may be the most important strategy you use to deliver brand awareness and revenue results.

In addition, a relatively new idea has emerged called "account-based experience" (ABX). ABX goes beyond winning new customers and addresses the entire customer life cycle through on-boarding, cross-selling, upselling, and converting customers into evangelists.

As a result, a new model is emerging that combines ABM, ABX, and other account-based strategies, like influencer marketing, in B2B marketing.

We call this Total Customer Growth.

In short, Total Customer Growth is a system involving sales, marketing, and customer success (or whatever you call this team in your organization) to find, engage, convert, and grow profitable customers for life. It is a holistic approach to building a sustainable, long-term business model.

We wrote this book as a comprehensive practical guide to ABM, ABX, and Total Customer Growth. The book you hold includes how-tos, strategic rationales, examples, and references to resources to help in your journey.

It is divided into four parts:

- Part 1 reviews the concepts of the Total Customer Growth Model, including the strategic foundations of ABM.
- Part 2 gives you a practical guide for getting started with ABM as a first major step toward Total Customer Growth.
- Part 3 explains how to evolve from simply using ABM as an acquisition tool into the concepts of ABX and strategies to grow your existing customers.
- Part 4 paints a picture of how to steer your organization toward Total Customer Growth, the steps you should take, and how to get there.

We wrote this book to help you in many ways:

- If you are starting your ABM journey, we provide a comprehensive view of ABM and ABX, and introduce to a new concept called "Total Customer Growth."

- If you have been implementing ABM for some time, we hope this book gives you some new ideas about where you can take and better utilize this strategy.

- Lastly, if you or anyone on your team needs an instruction guide on any of the many areas of ABM and ABX, the book is designed so that you can dip into any chapter at any time to get a good foundation on topics like intent data, targeting, buyer journeys, etc.

We have endeavored to make this book applicable to your real world, using examples of the concepts put into practice with case studies and stories.

We have also created an online resource for you at https://learn. totalcustomergrowth.com. It is full of examples, templates, and tools you can use to put this book's theories and tips into action.

Every journey, no matter how big or small, starts with a first step. We hope this book will help you take an initial step, or your next step, toward Total Customer Growth.

Adam and Ben

Register at
https://learn.totalcustomergrowth.com
to access resources for this book.

PART 1

Strategic Foundations of Total Customer Growth

What You Will Learn in Part 1

This part of the book explains the principles of Total Customer Growth, ABM, and ABX. It also provides you with the strategic foundations on which you will build your Total Customer Growth strategy.

- In Chapter 1, you learn why ABM makes sense and why you need to become an expert in it.
- In Chapter 2, we introduce the Total Customer Growth Framework and how ABM and ABX are part of this model.
- Chapter 3 is all you ever wanted to know about intent data, the magic that powers ABM.
- Targeting is one of the most important foundations of ABM. In Chapter 4, we explain why and how to build an effective targeting model.
- In Chapter 5, we take you on the buyer journey. Understanding this well is critical to developing a sound ABM strategy.
- Chapter 6 reviews the different ABM campaign strategies and dives into why personalization matters.
- In Chapter 7, we give you a simple process for creating an engagement and content plan driven by what buyers need as they go through the journey.

CHAPTER 1

Why ABM Is Transforming B2B Sales and Marketing

What You Will Learn in This Chapter

- Why complex selling is so difficult and getting harder
- How companies buy and why they do not involve you until later in the process
- How the internet gives buyers greater control, and why this makes it harder to market to them
- What buyers need from you and how to meet their needs
- Why ABM is taking hold as a strategy
- Why you need to think about ABX, and what it is

Barriers in Complex Selling: The 5 Cs

If you have been selling B2B for a while, you may feel that it is getting harder, not easier, to engage buyers. You are not alone.

In a recent survey Adam's company conducted, nine out of ten technology sales and marketing executives said that in the last five years, selling and marketing technology products in complex sales situations has become more difficult.

Five reasons common across any industry:

- **Complexity** - Over the last few decades, markets have become increasingly complex. This is driven by many factors: consolidation, increasing competition, globalization, changing political climates, and, most recently, the pandemic. So, the stakes of any decision are much higher. Buyers have more factors to consider.

- **Consensus** - Gone are the days when you could close a deal on the golf course or simply get to the C-suite. Organizations are much more consensus-driven and appoint a buyer collective to evaluate solutions and recommend a decision. According to research conducted by CEB (formerly Corporate Executive Board), now part of Gartner, the average number of people in a buyer collective is 5.4. No doubt, in more-complex deals and in more risk-averse, regulated industries, buyer collectives can be much larger.

- **Compliance** - Every year, it feels like there are new rules, regulations, and standards. For example, in health care, you need to worry about HIPAA, anti-kickback legislation, and a host of security-compliance issues. This adds more time and complexity to the buying process.

- **Competition** - Very few markets are dominated by a handful of mega-players or the occasional duopoly. Instead, most markets are crammed with dozens of competitors fighting for market share, making the choice for a buyer collective overwhelming. For example, in recent interviews, we asked several health care executives about solutions they would consider for chronic care management, and each mentioned a completely different set of solutions.

- **Control** - Lastly, buyers are more in control of the buying process than ever. They do not need to engage with a vendor too early. Why? Information is widely available online. It is easy for buyers to educate themselves. They can easily compare solutions and talk with peers in various online forums. For a fee, they can buy analyst reports that help them decide. The net result is that they do not engage with vendors until much later in the process. According to Forrester, 67% of buyers form an opinion of a vendor before they engage one.

The Buyer Is in Control

So, what are they up to if they are not talking to you?

The Buyer Journey is not linear. It is a long, winding road on which the buyer researches and discusses issues with colleagues and third parties long before they engage with you.

Typically, a buyer starts with initial research online, most likely to explore the problem and how others have solved it. Purchasers reach out to their peers for advice and possibly look across an extended network via social media. Doing so gives them a set of vendors to explore (hopefully, including you). Armed with this list and a partially formed impression about what they need to buy, they then visit your website--and your competitors' websites.

At this point, they are looking for a great deal of specific information. We hear buyers say they prefer to learn about your solution on their own before engaging with you directly. They expect you to provide that information online and explain how you have solved their problem before.

After gathering all this information, they meet with the buying committee.

And then, maybe, just maybe, they fill out an online form to be contacted, request a personalized demo, watch a product video, or download a customer case study.

Figuring out what a buyer's journey truly looks like is a dark art. We all know that there is no such thing as a typical buyer journey. Every organization buys differently. Moreover, there are multiple people in a buyer collective, each with their own interests and buying behaviors.

But Buyers Do Need Your Help

In their book *The Challenger Customer: Selling to the Hidden Influencer Who Can Multiply Your Results*, Brent Adamson and his colleagues refer to a study on buyer behavior across 3,000 B2B buyers. One of the most interesting findings relates to what they call "buyer dysfunction."

In their study, they asked B2B buyers to rate how difficult decisions were made throughout a buying process. There are three stages to selecting a vendor:

1. Problem definition
2. Solution definition
3. Vendor evaluation

According to the *The Challenger Customer*, B2B buyers report that defining the solution is the hardest part of the process for the buyer collective. Their research showed that 35% of buyers report that defining the problem as a group was the hardest part of their buying process. However, 50% report that defining how they will solve the problem was hardest for them to resolve. Curiously only 27% said that selecting a vendor was the hardest issue for the buyer collective to agree on.

Moreover, the research also showed that buyer collectives find it three times harder to decide on how they will solve a problem than on who they will select to help them solve this.

The bad news is that buyers do not typically engage directly with a vendor until much later in the process. The good news, though, is that they need a great deal of help.

So, if you can get the right type of information in front of them at the right time—when they are researching the problem and how to solve it—you have a better chance of getting on the short list of vendors they will speak with.

If you are smart, you will figure out how to jump to the head of the line and help define the requirements the buyer is looking for.

This is where ABM, ABX, and Total Customer Growth come in.

As we explain in the introduction, ABM has become primarily associated with generating demand. It is also a strategy for improving brand awareness and increasing revenue.

ABX is a relatively new idea that goes beyond winning new customers. Definitions vary, but the primary principle of ABX is that it encompasses how you grow revenue from existing customers.

As a result, a new model is emerging that combines ABM, ABX, and other account-based strategies, like influencer marketing in B2B marketing. In short, Total Customer Growth involves sales, marketing, and customer success to find, engage, convert, and grow profitable customers for life. It is a holistic approach to building a sustainable, long-term business approach.

Why ABM Is Taking Hold

There are many definitions of ABM. In our view, it is about three things:

- Identifying accounts that are in-market for your solution
- Focusing attention on the accounts that are the best fit for you
- Targeting the buyer collective in a very personalized way

You can use intent data to identify who is in-market. We dive into this more deeply later in the book. Intent data is like magic that provides signals about accounts that are researching information related to the problem you solve. There are many easy-to-ascertain intent tools, but third-party sources—like Bombora, a leading provider of ABM intent data—have gained a great deal of attention.

Based on these signals, you can narrow down which prospects on your target account list (TAL) should get the most attention and investment. You can then run marketing and sales campaigns you tailor to these accounts with greater precision than a mass campaign aimed at your entire TAL.

For example, the entire hospital provider market may be fair game for your solution if you are selling a virtual care hospital solution. However, you can use intent data to ascertain that only 5% of hospitals are actively researching this topic and have the intent to buy this year.

So, rather than spending time, marketing dollars, and sales resources to try to reach the entire market with a generalized message, you can develop a precisely targeted and aggressively focused campaign to the 5% actually in-market to purchase.

This difference is profound. It means you will focus your marketing resources on 5% of the market, rather than casting a wide net across its entirety in the hopes of reaching accounts that may be interested.

And it truly works.

Here is a real-world example from a health care B2B SaaS software company targeting midsize to large health care providers in North America.

The company knew their target market in detail when it came to the buyer personas, target hospitals, competitive landscape, and compelling events. What they did not know before ABM was when a hospital was in the market for a new computerized maintenance management system (CMMS) that the clinical engineers would use to track repairs and maintenance of medical devices. Hospitals typically replace this software every five to ten years, so timing is everything.

In the past, this specific health care company pulled a targeted list of hospitals that matched their ideal customer profile (ICP), then began marketing outreach, sales development representative calls, and sales relationship building. Unfortunately, they wasted significant money, time, and effort on accounts that had no current buying interest. Less than 5% of the customers contacted progressed past an introduction call and high-level product demonstration.

This is exactly where ABM changed the game. The SaaS company stood up intent data with Bombora and a digital ABM product to deliver targeted digital ads to hospitals that showed buying intent.

Using this process, when the marketing team sent targeted ads, they focused resources on the accounts that had some level of interest in topics relevant to a buying decision. For example, if a hospital started to show interest in the term *CMMS*, the SaaS company served specific ads and emails focused on that topic. Once an account showed enough interest, went to the SaaS company's website, and converted to a lead, the SaaS company had an SDR call into the hospital and the specific prospect.

In this way, every effort the SaaS company put into its marketing and sales efforts was directed at hospitals in the buying or information-gathering process related to the software products that this SaaS company could provide.

The saying "Work smarter, not harder" is accurate when it comes to leveraging ABM as part of the foundation for your marketing, sales, and customer success approach. After moving to this model, this SaaS company saw over 50% of its warm outreach make it past a discovery call and demonstration, since there was *real* interest from these hospitals.

Why ABX Is the Next Big Thing

If you have been using ABM as a better way to generate demand, now is the time to think bigger, not only about how you can use the principles of ABM to acquire customers, but how ABM can underpin a better end-to-end growth model.

This is what ABX does.

So, what the heck is ABX?

Demandbase defines it as "a go-to-market strategy that uses data and insights to orchestrate relevant, trusted marketing and sales actions throughout the B2B customer journey."

Terminus defines it as "a holistic approach to account-based marketing, making it a business philosophy more than just a marketing philosophy. Under ABX, everything is done to personalize and tailor services to the individual client, leading to much higher rates of acquisition and retention, better word of mouth, and vastly improved ROI."

ABX is far more than just marketing. It is, in essence, a business philosophy that covers the whole customer journey.

ABX includes the practices involved in ABM techniques to acquire customers, but it goes beyond them. It includes how you grow and retain those customers once you have acquired them and how you turn them into evangelists for your business. It also includes identifying at-risk customers and getting them back on track.

Here is a real-world example of how a B2B SaaS company used ABX to expand the use of its products to its existing customer base and deliver net new revenue as a result.

This B2B SaaS company sells software products focused on equipment maintenance, facilities, and workplace solutions. It sold one of its initial products to almost every one of its customers. Since that point, the company had created several additional products that those existing customers could also take advantage of.

In the past, customer success worked directly with the account's existing champion or product owner and discussed these new products. In many cases, that champion or product owner would not know who would use these new products or who had responsibility for the business areas that could benefit from them.

In those cases, a new pursuit was needed to find the additional stakeholders and sell into those departments. Prior to ABX, the challenge was that there was no real data for understanding the current intent and needs in those business units.

When COVID hit, many of this company's existing customers needed space and workplace solutions. But they didn't know which ones.

This is exactly where ABX played a key role. By leveraging Bombora data and applying it to the existing customer base in the Customer Relationship Management system (CRM), customer success team members could see which existing accounts were showing intent signals for space and workplace solutions. This also included intent for competitors in the market to know which existing accounts were looking at competitors, even though there was a solution already available on a platform they had already deployed.

By leveraging this data, customer success teams could directly target customers that showed buying intent for one of the unused products and sell them another product on a platform they already had running. This saved the customer time and money while also solving their problem.

This real-world example shows the full life cycle of a customer journey and increased revenue for the business.

• • •

In the next chapter, we go into the Total Customer Growth Framework. This new model could underpin the way your company sells, markets, and serves customers. It could also drive your product development.

Are you ready to take the first step toward Total Customer Growth?

Register at
https://learn.totalcustomergrowth.com to access resources for this chapter including the Total Customer Growth Planning Framework. You can use it as you read this book.

CHAPTER 2

The Total Customer Growth Framework

What You Will Learn in This Chapter

- Why you need to think about the whole buyer journey and why ABM and ABX currently do not address this
- What the total buyer journey is and why it is a different way of thinking about B2B marketing
- An introduction to the Total Customer Growth Framework
- How the Total Customer Growth Framework works in practice

Buyer journeys are helpful ways of thinking about the process an individual and a buyer committee or buyer collective goes through to buy a solution.

The problem with these buyer journeys is that they are incomplete.

As sales and marketing people, we tend to think the customer journey ends when the deal is signed. To us, this is the finish line. But to our customers, this is the starting point. When a buyer goes through the whole process, they are not thinking about the job being done when they select you as their partner. They look at this as the start of a long-term relationship.

If this were a marriage, it is as if we think about developing a relationship only up until the wedding. After that, it is someone else's problem. Our customers think of the wedding day (the signed deal) as the start of a marriage (the long-term relationship).

The Total Buyer Journey

We propose a complete way of looking at the buyer journey, which is the way a buyer thinks about their relationship with you.

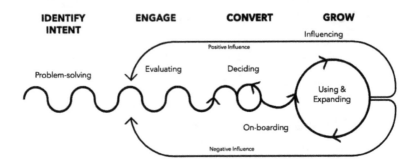

You can see that the middle wavy arrow starts with the typical buyer journey stages, where buyers define the problem and how to solve it. Next, they evaluate vendors and make a decision.

Then, they go through an on-boarding process to learn how to use your solution, integrate it with other systems, train their teams, and grow adoption. They are then using the solution day-to-day (hopefully). As your solution becomes embedded in their organization, they expand their use. This expansion includes adding more users, adding features, upgrading, etc.

Lastly, as they use your solution and work with your firm, they develop opinions about you and share those with others. This influence can be negative, neutral, or positive.

What's Different?

Organizations tend to think and act in silos. Marketing is primarily responsible for the early part of the buyer journey, sales is responsible for the middle, and customer success is responsible for the relationship after the deal is closed.

ABM supports the marketing and sales stages. And over the last decade, it has proven to be a very effective strategy. ABX is primarily about helping you grow your existing business. We go into how shortly.

This changes the focus from new customer acquisition to lifetime customer value. It changes the way sales, marketing, and customer success operate. **It puts as much value on customer satisfaction as it does on sales.** And it puts as much attention on turning customers into positive advocates as it does on generating demand. It also emphasizes the marketing's role in helping upsell.

Lastly, Total Customer Growth is about thinking, finding, and growing highly profitable relationships with the right customers.

As a marketer, what does not change is that you are focused on **getting the right message in front of the right customer at the right time.**

The Total Customer Growth Framework

If you have investigated or are already practicing ABM, you are familiar with the ABM framework. There are several variations on this, but the typical stages are:

1. Target
2. Engage
3. Convert
4. Optimize

We propose a new model: The Total Customer Growth Framework. The idea is that the principles of ABM are as important to the relationship with a customer after a sale as when the customer is only a prospect. There are four distinct stages to this model:

1. **Identify Intent** - You identify which best-fit prospect accounts are in-market for your solution
2. **Engage** - You help these prospects conclude that you should be considered and facilitate contact through an orchestrated marketing program
3. **Convert** - You continue to engage the prospect to convert into a sale
4. **Grow** - You monitor customer satisfaction and intent for other solutions, upsell them, and convert them into evangelists for your business

The fundamental principles of ABM do not change, but they are applied differently. For example, you use intent data to determine which prospective accounts are in-market. Additionally, you use intent data to identify other solutions your current customers are interested in.

You use what you learn about your most profitable and most highly regarded customers to refine your definition of a best-fit customer so that you can improve how you target equally profitable new customers.

Personalization is even more important. Your current customers expect to be recognized and treated differently. As you market to them, it will be critical to acknowledge them and show that you know them.

Total Customer Growth in Action

To illustrate, here are four examples of Total Customer Growth in action where ABM principles are part of a more holistic, long-term relationship. We have kept all firms' names anonymous to protect their confidentiality.

Intent in Action

Company A is a multibillion-dollar technology and services business that has relationships with most large financial institutions. This company has expanded its portfolio of solutions by acquiring other businesses.

One of its most recent acquisitions was a novel technology solution in credit card services. Our consulting team designed a pilot for Company A using third-party intent data with the goal of using this intent data with their current customer list to see which ones could be in-market for these additional services.

On day one of a pilot using intent data, the SDRs identified that one major customer in the Northeast was showing high intent for credit card services. The SDR lead contacted the account manager in charge of this relationship. They pinpointed the stakeholder responsible for credit card services, then scheduled a call.

During the call, this key stakeholder told the account manager that they would shortly issue a Request for Proposal (RFP) and that they had not been aware that Company A provided credit card services. As a result of the call, the firm was included in the RFP.

The SDR team generated 60 meetings using this technique—half with existing customers and half with net new accounts—and closed over $3 million in new sales over the next six months. The ROI was 50 times.

Engagement in Action

Prospect A is a midsize convenience store that was actively working to select a new facilities maintenance solution. They met with their main technology advisory agency to determine which vendors to include in an RFP. As part of this process, both the agency and Prospect A were visiting Company X's website to view customer case studies and testimonials, as they were considering Company X's solution and several other competitors to include in the RFP. Once Company X saw Prospect A was showing intent on the website, it initiated targeted advertising on social media, websites, and emails to make sure the buyer collective knew why it should be included in the RFP.

Company X was included on the RFP and won the business six months later. Company X made sure its brand and key content were specific and targeted to address this account's business needs and was able to share the specific messages and content to Prospect A them make their selection.

Conversion in Action

Prospect B is a Fortune 5000 global retailer working on launching new corporate headquarters. One of Company X's account executives (AEs) was pursuing Prospect B and had a strong relationship with the champion in the account. Company X had a key value proposition that the competition could not match. As their solution was built on a technology platform the retailer used and Company X knew how to support it, they felt they were well-positioned. They just needed a way to accelerate the deal to avoid the risk of a no-decision (i.e., continuing to do things the way they always had). Company X was also concerned that this project's budget could be eliminated. Their team was focused on closing the deal quickly.

Company X set up a personalized landing page and content built specifically for Prospect B. This content was designed to get them to showcase that Company X could meet their business objectives and demonstrate the financial value of doing so sooner than later, which included incorporating a business value assessment in the content.

With targeted and personalized content focused on business value, Company X closed the deal two months ahead of the expected deadline. The champion in the account was able to use this personalized content with their executive team to justify why making this purchase now made sense.

Growth in Action

Company D is a marketing services firm that specializes in digital marketing. They won a new account with a Fortune 500 financial services firm. This client worked with several agencies, and Company D was one of the smallest firms they worked with.

At the end of its first year, Company D ran a satisfaction survey across the client. This included a Net Promoter Score-like survey that went to several dozen clients and in-depth interviews with a handful of executives.

Company D used this information to develop a growth plan for this client. This included understanding additional needs, pinpointing needed improvements, inviting clients to be panelists at events with Company D, and publishing case studies.

This process was repeated annually and informed a long-term growth plan that resulted in ten times more growth in revenues from this client over five years.

● ● ●

In the rest of this book, we provide a step-by-step process showing you how to implement Total Customer Growth across your organization. The first step is about finding who has intent.

In the next chapter, we dive into ABM's secret sauce, AKA intent data. This can be remarkably powerful if you know how to use it. We will help you understand this better.

> Go to https://learn.totalcustomergrowth.com to access resources for this chapter including the Total Customer Growth Planning Framework. You can use it as you read this book.

CHAPTER 3

Starting with Intent

What You Will Learn in This Chapter

- What intent data is and why you need to use it
- What the different types of intent data are and how you capture it
- What buying signals are and how you use them
- Six examples of intent data in action
- How third-party intent data is sourced

One of the sexiest things in ABM is intent data.

It is like magic!

Used effectively, it can boost your marketing effectiveness, but it is still a bit of a mystery to many B2B marketers, so let's start with a definition.

To put it in the context of the Total Customer Growth Model, this chapter is key to becoming an expert in the Identify Intent stage.

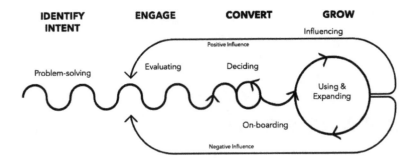

What Exactly Is Intent Data?

According to Bombora, intent data is information collected about a web user's observed behavior—specifically web content consumption—that provides insights into their interests. This insight often indicates potential intent to take a specific action.

The short story is that there are three types of ABM intent data:

- **First-party intent data** - This is information your company captures on its website and social media channels that signals that a company may have an intention to buy your product. Examples are visiting your solutions page multiple times, downloading a buyer guide, or signing up for a webinar.

- **Second-party intent data** - This includes review sites, like Capterra and G2, which compare different companies within a category and include customer ratings. These sites sell leads from interested buyers.

- **Third-party intent data** - This is data provided by a third party, like ZoomInfo or Bombora. It provides signals on buying intent by companies from third-party websites. For example, a prospect downloaded a white paper about your product category on a trade magazine website. The third-party intent data vendors have relationships with thousands of third parties, and they aggregate the buying behavior of millions of buyers for thousands of topics.

Why Is It Important to Use Intent Data?

For most of the buyer journey, the buyers are researching on their own, talking to peers, and interacting on social media. It is only late in the process that they interact with you. By then, they have well-informed opinions and may have already decided the company they are going to buy from.

This is where intent data comes in. Intent data gives you business intelligence about who is in-market for your solution, who is out there researching the categories you operate in, how you can help them solve a problem, what their options are, and who they should consider, including your competitors.

It can tell you which accounts you need to focus on in your prospecting and marketing. Because one of the key principles of ABM is focusing on a small number of best-fit targets, intent data helps you determine who those are.

Intent data in B2B marketing can be an unfair advantage if you use it strategically!

How Do You Source Intent Data?

The number of sources of intent data is constantly increasing. Bombora is the best known. It is all they do, and they have been at it a long time. ZoomInfo acquired a third-party intent data provider you can access through the ZoomInfo platform. Both charge an annual fee.

If you purchase an ABM platform—like 6sense, Terminus, or Demandbase—ABM intent data is integrated into the platform. In most cases, these platforms can incorporate a variety of intent signals, including third-party data from Bombora.

You can also license Bombora and ZoomInfo intent data independently. You can easily integrate it with your CRM or marketing automation system. This way, you can see intent signals in the sales and marketing systems you use day-to-day.

One important note: Most sources of intent data provide only account-level information. They do this for privacy reasons. It would be more helpful to know which specific individual at a company is interested in what you do, but that would be a privacy violation. Most sales and marketing teams have other tools and data sources to start identifying the individuals once they know what accounts to focus on.

Buying Signals: Intent Data in Action

Third-party intent data provides signals about which accounts are actively interested in specific topics. Think of topics as search terms.

Here is an example based on one of our clients, a virtual care provider especially interested in finding telehealth buyers. We licensed Bombora integrated with HubSpot, which is increasingly useful for ABM. Bombora offered a dozen relevant topics related to telehealth. We set up a report in Bombora's application that dynamically searched for health care provider organizations interested in those topics.

Using the integration, our client could easily see which accounts were showing buying intent for telehealth topics.

Bombora provides a company Surge Score® for each topic that reflects how actively a company is researching that topic. The Bombora Rollup Average Score is an average of the scores for all the relevant topics a company is researching. The Bombora Rollup Count of Topics shows how many relevant topics the company is searching for, and the adjacent column shows which topics are of interest to that company.

And it works. Here is a testimonial about Bombora:

> Bombora's company surge data enables us to know (not guess) when companies are in market. When we know what the customer is interested in, our marketing campaigns can become more specific, targeted, and helpful in the buyer's journey. Salespeople also have enjoyed using the data to know what products and solutions are relevant to the customer—without even having a conversation with them.

Note: ZoomInfo provides similar information.

Intent Data Use Cases

You can do a lot with intent data. Here are several examples of the use of intent data, from the simple to the more complex.

1. In-Market Alerts for Sales Teams

One of the simplest uses of intent data is providing in-market reports to your sales team, especially SDRs. You can do this by integrating the source of intent data with your CRM.

The key is to make it easy for SDRs to access it in the system they use as part of their daily activity (e.g., Salesforce).

If you also integrate this with your web analytics, the dashboard will display how an account may be in-market and what their activity on your website is. For an SDR with hundreds of accounts to target, this is invaluable information, as it helps them prioritize where to hunt.

According to one Chief Marketing Officer (CMO):

> Basically, we can see if our buyers are potentially out there looking for something that would fit what we sell. So, if someone's out there looking at one of our competitors, for example, or looking at medical device maintenance software, we actually can leverage data around that to be able to help target our buyers that are actually currently looking for a solution. And by the way, it is not just intent data. It is also intended based on job titles. So, we can actually look at a couple of different angles of that data to be able to help us prioritize not only with our BDR/SDR organization but also with sales. It says here's potential accounts that are showing intent and looking for solutions either in your space or in your competitor's landscape.

2. At-Risk Customers

While the most exciting use of intent data is finding new customers, it is also valuable in keeping an eye on existing ones.

For example, if you are in a wireless networking company, you can create a report that tracks what your customers are interested in. If you see that they are actively surging for wireless networking as a topic or looking at your competitors' websites, it may indicate that they are looking around.

Equally, you can use intent data with your existing accounts to identify when they are showing intent for other services you offer.

3. Segment-Specific Sales Routines

Once your SDRs are familiar with intent data, it may be time to move up to a segment-specific approach to ABM. In segment-specific, or 1:Few, ABM, you market to a group of accounts with commonalities.

For example, if you are selling telecommunications services and notice that prospects tend to be interested in cloud VOIP, hosted VOIP, and IP telephony, you can develop separate marketing sequences for each topic. Each week, you segment prospects based on interest in each topic (e.g., the highest surging, respectively, for cloud VOIP, hosted VOIP, and IP telephony). You then create lists of target contacts for each segment and run the appropriate segment-specific sequence against each segment.

4. Intent-Based Display Advertising

One of the coolest uses of intent data is targeting your advertising to in-market prospects.

The ABM platforms, like RollWorks and Terminus, make it easy to run orchestrated digital ad campaigns to in-market targets. Part of this is running targeted display ads through their own demand-side platform (DSP) network. For example, if you are selling security services, you specify topics related to security and run digital ads that are displayed exclusively to people from companies that are showing high interest in the topic. These ads run across Terminus's display ad network.

One of my favorite uses of intent data is how you can use it with LinkedIn. This is quite simple. Again, as in the case of the security software firm, you would run a weekly report through your intent data service to identify companies that appear to be in-market for security software. You then export this as a list into LinkedIn Campaign Manager. (With some services, LinkedIn can be integrated so this can happen automatically.)

You then run a campaign targeting specific relevant titles (e.g., CISOs) at companies in-market with content or an offer that is relevant to the topic of highest interest (e.g., malware threats).

5. Using Intent Data In Content Marketing

Lastly, intent data can be valuable in helping shape your content strategy.

For example, a Target Account List (TAL) appears to have a high interest in asset management and security orchestration. As asset management is a core part of what this company offers, they have marketing materials and content. Security orchestration is a newly surging topic. The sales team alerts marketing about this, and together they develop new content specifically geared toward security orchestration.

How Well Does Third-Party Intent Data Cover Your Market?

The value of intent data is a factor of the number of topics covered. And the number of topics is expanding all the time. As a customer of Bombora, you can request that new intent topics be added to grow the scope of the topics they cover for your market.

Bombora covers over 10,000 topics and growing, as organizations continue to request that new topics be added. Periodically—typically quarterly—you should review your topics and either request new ones or review any new ones they have already added. This should be an ongoing process as part of your ABM program so you can stay current with your topics and what is relevant in your market. You can also make this procedure part of your ongoing SEO optimization.

As you see keywords ranking for SEO, you should also consider those as part of your ABM strategy.

Note: ZoomInfo covers around 4,000 topics. This list is growing all the time.

●   ●   ●

In the next chapter, we cover something that may seem familiar—targeting. But you will need to take a different and more evolved approach in building a successful Total Customer Growth and ABM Model. The next chapter explains why and how.

> Go to https://learn.totalcustomergrowth.com
> to access resources for this chapter including
> a reference to different types of intent data.

CHAPTER 4

Targeting

What You Will Learn in This Chapter

- Why targeting with ABM is different from traditional B2B marketing
- Why defining your ideal customer profile (ICP) is so important in ABM
- What the characteristics of an ICP are
- How you can use these characteristics to create a better ICP definition
- How you can then build a better TAL designed for ABM
- How to score accounts for ABM, and a real-world example

Targeting is incredibly important when it comes to ABM, even more important than it is in traditional B2B marketing because with ABM, you focus your resources on fewer targets and commit to a much more personalized approach to marketing. It is like spearfishing versus a traditional wide-net approach.

There is, however, a risk. If you get the TAL wrong, you place the wrong bet. That is why it is critical to do your homework and thoroughly plan the approach.

This affects the entire Total Customer Growth Model. In the Identify Intent and Engage stages, it will help make your demand generation more effective. In terms of conversion, you should also see larger deals. Lastly, your growth of current customers will be more successful, as you have acquired customers that are ideal for what you do.

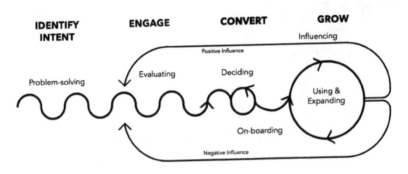

Differences Between Traditional and ABM Targeting

There are some differences between the more traditional approach to targeting and how targeting has evolved with ABM. In the old way, we focused on territories. That is still an understandable way to divide up your sales. But there is a much greater focus on the TAL rather than geography.

The old way is a wide-net approach that uses a mass outreach to your TAL; the new way is targeted spearfishing to accounts in your customer segment that are showing actual buying intent.

In the old way, there was a conveyor-belt handoff between sales and marketing, where a marketing qualified lead (MQL) was handed off to somebody on the sales team to qualify, so it became a sales-qualified lead (SQL).

In this new way, you and your team work together much more collaboratively across marketing and sales by driving awareness and interest in an automated way before sales gets engaged in the process.

The ICP Is Critical

The ideal customer profile (ICP) is an important tool for any B2B marketer. It is even more important in ABM.

In short, an ICP, sometimes known as an ideal buyer profile, defines your perfect customer. This is a fictitious company that has all the qualities that make them the best fit for the solutions you provide. You may have multiple ICPs. For example:

- Large regional financial services organizations with over $10 billion in assets
- Large national networks of financial advisors
- Regional networks of financial advisors

Characteristics of an ICP

1. Customers with High Revenue Potential

Targets, prospects, or customers with the highest revenue potential are ideal for your business growth. What do they look like?

These customers have the greatest need and the budgets to solve these issues. Seems obvious, right? The trick is NOT spending time on customers that have less need and do not have the wherewithal to buy from you.

2. Shorter Average Sales Cycles

Given how long sales cycles in B2B selling can last, this is an even more important attribute. This is more a wish than anything else, as it is very hard to target based on this. But as you develop your strategy, take the time to consider what might make some organizations buy faster than others. For example, they buy faster when they have just acquired or merged with a new company, and there is an urgent need to integrate the organizations.

The size of an organization can sometimes be a factor too, as we discuss next. We sometimes refer to these as Goldilocks customers. They are not so small that they lack the budget to buy what you offer, but they are also not so big that the sales cycle will last forever.

3. Best-Fit Industry Segment

This is harder than it sounds. Typically, there are obvious macro segments of industries in your target market, but which micro segment should you pursue?

There is an art to deciding this.

When creating the ICP for his clinical communications business, Uniphy Health, Adam determined that their solution was best suited to large regional health care systems. These were smaller than national health systems but larger than a three-to-four hospital system. It took time to understand this, but once they did, they focused on these two targets with precision.

4. Geographical Location (where applicable)

This attribute is determined by your ability to serve, such as selling a service that depends on having people in specific locations to serve local customers. Geography will be less important for companies not limited by location, such as an SaaS business whose customers do not need onsite support.

Another factor may be the stage of your business. In the early days of Adam's health care technology software firm, Uniphy Health, they decided to focus on customers they could serve within driving distance so they could build great references through high-touch service. In the first two years, they sold and served customers exclusively in the Northeast region of the US. Once they established this beachhead, they expanded based on their sales network's reach.

5. Aligned with Your Company's Objectives

Finally, is the prospect a fit for you? This may seem obvious, but it is actually tricky. For example, if one of your objectives is to be the leader in your field, it will be key to have references from the top firms in your market. If your objective is to be seen as an innovator, seeking out the most innovative customers will be important.

Important Note

As you go through this process, addressability is a critical factor. Can you source data to help you pinpoint customers that meet these attributes? As a simple filter, as you determine the criteria of your ICP, ask yourself a question: "Can I source data that will allow me to filter customers based on these criteria?"

How to Narrow Down Your ICP

Developing your ICP is about draining the swamp—eliminating the wrong targets to reveal the right targets. The trick is to remove prospects that are unlikely to become profitable customers. As you refine your ICP, develop a set of disqualifying criteria.

Here are some examples.

1. Financial Viability and Stability

If your target customer is not financially stable or is in the process of being acquired, you cannot rely on them for future business.

2. Ability to Sell to Them

You may aspire to have the market leader as your customer, but they may be incredibly hard to sell to. If you do not have the right people on your team and cannot withstand very long sales cycles, selling to organizations like this is not for you.

3. Relationships

Do you have relationships you can leverage? If no one in your organization has a relationship with a potential prospect, maybe you should eliminate that prospect from current consideration.

4. Competitors

Obviously, you need to know if a prospect uses your competitor's product. In some cases, that might disqualify them. For example, if they recently purchased your competitor's solution, they will not be ready to switch.

Equally, if they have had your competitor for a while, they may be more open to switching. The key is to eliminate from consideration prospects that are already satisfied customers.

5. Third-Party-Related Barriers

What third-party issues disqualify the prospect from consideration? In some markets, their financial system may be important. Their electronic health record (EHR) system is an important consideration in health care. Epic customers are known for their zealous loyalty. However, Adam found that organizations that had been Epic customers for a while were often easier to sell to than recent Epic customers.

He found that the longer-standing Epic customers valued them for many reasons but were often frustrated by the time it took to get a specific feature. That weakness opened them up to offers from outside the Epic tent.

Building a TAL

Once you have this all figured out, it is time to build a TAL. There are many different sources of data, including ZoomInfo and Definitive Healthcare. The trick is to source data that will enable you to use the ICP (ideal customer profile) criteria in an addressable way.

This means you can create a TAL that meets your ICP criteria as closely as possible.

Your initial list may be sufficiently targeted. This is where TAL scoring comes in.

How to Score Your TAL for Best-Fit Accounts

After successfully creating your TAL, you need to know how to score it to determine your best-fit accounts.

What Is TAL Scoring?

It is the process of prioritizing your already created TAL into a shorter list of accounts that present you with the greatest opportunity.

TAL scoring enables your organization to effectively channel its efforts and resources to only the best-fit accounts with high purchase potential.

Traditional TAL Scoring

This is a systematic account scoring process that begins by going through your list of accounts and taking it through a scoring framework.

For instance, if your company is doing well with midsize Goldilocks accounts (not too big, not too small) that use a technology you integrate well with, give those accounts higher scores than larger organizations using another system.

Scoring Criteria

Each company will have its method of account scoring that depends on the nature of its business. The key is to develop a systematic framework that reflects your best practice in identifying best-fit accounts.

You will determine filters that allow you to use data to prioritize or deprioritize accounts. There are four criteria to use in this process:

1. Firmographics

This allows you to segment your target accounts based on traditional business attributes. Typical attributes include the number of employees, number of beds, revenues, locations, market segment, geography, etc.

2. Sales History

With this criterion, you filter accounts based on your history with them. For example, lapsed lead, active lead, or former customer.

3. Positioning Attribute

This is a critical step. It is when you apply key filters based on your business's unique characteristics. For example, which financial system a prospect uses, your ability to integrate, and the current incumbent competitor.

It might also include the strength or vulnerability of an incumbent vendor that you are trying to displace. This is the criterion you want to spend the most time on.

4. Behavior

Behavior is where intent data comes in. We cover this in detail in future chapters. Intent data indicates how actively an account is considering a purchase.

Are they in-market? This includes how actively they engage on your website, the content they download, and the videos they watch.

Weighting TAL Scoring

You then need to adopt a weighting score technique. It is based on the relative importance of the scoring criteria in your scoring framework.

You compute the scores accordingly to get weighted percentages for account prioritization. This traditional TAL scoring model works well and keeps your accounts organized.

Modern TAL Scoring

With the advent of artificial intelligence (AI) in marketing, scoring and qualifying accounts is becoming much more data driven. TALs are optimized in real time. For example, one new dynamic technique called "FIRE scoring" is Demandbase's proprietary approach.

FIRE stands for account **F**it, **I**ntent, **R**elationships, and level of **E**ngagement.

You can now develop a predictive model on your own by leveraging the data from your CRM, layering on intent data to identify who actually might be in-market, looking at existing relationships, and analyzing website engagement metrics to identify potential customers

Case Study: Developing an ICP for B2B Health Care Marketing

This is a case study on how Uniphy Health developed its ICP for B2B health care marketing and reflects Adam's own experience in creating our ICP in our second year in business.

Adam's story:

In 2012, I founded a health care technology firm with a physician and a software developer. We had some initial success. Within two years, we were in a growing but very crowded market with over 100 competitors; we needed to be strategic in approaching the market and who we targeted. Our ability to customize our solutions to suit our target customers' needs made us stand out.

Because of this customization, we could command an average deal size of $250,000. So, our ability to customize was our key differentiator, and we needed to be as precise as possible in how we found best-fit accounts for this offering. We started by segmenting our target market into hospitals, physicians, and clinically integrated networks. Later, we included accountable care organizations (ACOs) and large physician groups.

After identifying our market segment, we developed an ICP process to find Goldilocks customers. This was a strategic decision because we knew that sales cycles for large customers could be as long as two years.

On the other hand, we felt that small organizations did not have the budget or financial capacity to suit our desired deal size. Initially, we filtered our target customers based on the following:

Our first filter was the organization's size. To begin, we focused on two segments: health care systems and independent hospitals. Our primary targets were large regional health care systems. These were typically 5-to-15 hospital systems that served part of their state. For example, Hackensack Meridian Health and RWJBarnabas Health in New Jersey.

We also included large independent hospitals as well as academic medical centers. One such example of the Goldilocks hospitals we targeted was Winthrop. It is now part of NYU Langone Hospital in Long Island, but at the time, it was independent.

Initially, we limited ourselves to customers we could drive to. We felt it was important to be on-site as often as possible, so we focused our activities on accounts within a 100 miles radius. These included customers in the Northeast and Mid-Atlantic regions. We took a very high-touch approach in our sales.

Later, as we grew our sales staff and took on resellers, we expanded our geographic footprint.

The Other ICP Characteristics

1. Seeking Financial Strength

The other characteristic we considered when developing our ICP (B2B health care) was the financial strength of our target accounts. If they were not financially strong, they were unlikely to come up with $250,000 for our solution.

2. Initially Avoiding Epic Customers in Our Health Care B2B ICP

Epic was the leading electronic health care record vendor. This may sound counterintuitive, given Epic's importance, but it took us three years to find an opportunity to integrate our solution with Epic. Without those credentials, selling to an Epic customer was very tough sledding.

Initially, when creating our ICP for health care B2B, we prioritized customers of Cerner and Siemens (now actually part of Cerner), as we had the best references for these.

3. Excluding Customers in Merger Talks

When developing an ICP for our B2B health care customers, we excluded health care systems that were in merger talks or rumored to be a target.

4. Excluding Accounts Buying Competitor Products from Our B2B ICP

At that time, the market was still fairly new, so there was not much churn. If an account had bought our competitor's product in the last year, we deprioritized them, as they would be unlikely to switch. But one competitor in particular had a very poor reputation. We found that after a year, many customers were open to switching.

5. Getting Introduced to the Chief Medical Officer

Another softer filter was our ability to engage with the chief medical officer. My partner was a physician, giving us additional credibility with these hard-to-reach people. He was very adept at getting ahold of them.

6. Including Innovation Bias in Our B2B ICP

And lastly, we gave priority to customers we felt had an innovative mindset. These health care systems seemed open to working with startups. To identify suitable customers, we analyzed some of the firms they worked with that we could easily compare ourselves to.

This process worked well for us and gave us great early momentum in a competitive market with long sales cycles.

Once you have defined your target market and your way to identify ideal customers, the next stage is to understand how they buy.

• • •

The next chapter reviews the buyer journey. To be candid, this is something that most firms do badly or at least very superficially. When done well, however, the buyer journey can be the most powerful tool in your strategic arsenal. It will guide how you develop effective campaigns.

Sounds important, right?

Go to https://learn.totalcustomergrowth.com
to access resources for this chapter
including a Target Account List Checklist.

CHAPTER 5

The Buyer Journey

What You Will Learn in This Chapter

- How to define and map the buyer collective
- How to create a persona and why that is only the start of creating a useful buyer journey
- Why you need to dedicate time and resources to understanding the champion persona's needs and questions at the different stages of the buyer journey
- How to create a detailed buyer journey that maps their needs and questions, how they search for information, how to identify their buying signals, and what sources they trust
- How to synthesize all this information into a prioritized list of issues to focus on

So, you have defined the best-fit customers and started to build and refine your TAL. Now, though, you need to go deeper and build the next level in your Total Customer Growth strategy—defining the buyer journey.

The approach we review next is designed to map this process from the buyer's point of view:

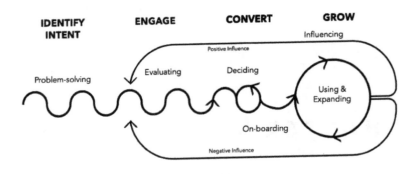

The buyer journey helps you understand how the individuals at your target accounts buy solutions like yours. This knowledge will frame how you develop your plan to identify in-market accounts, engage individual buyers, and convert them into customers. If they are already customers, it will help you frame how to expand your business with them.

In this process, you start by defining the buyer collective—the individual roles within a target account who are involved in buying decisions—and develop personas for the key individuals. For each persona, you map out their issues as they go through a buying process, what information they need, what they search for online, and what sources of information they trust.

The Buyer Collective

There are many individuals involved in complex sales. As explained in Chapter 1, an average of 5.4 people are involved in a buying process. In markets where consensus-driven decision-making is even more of a factor, the number may be much larger.

Here is a typical buyer collective:

Buyer Collective

CFO COO CEO

VP of Customer Support   Compliance VP   CIO/CTO   VP of Banking Product Management   VP of Call Center Ops

Influencer   Decision maker   Champion

In simple terms, there are three types of stakeholders:

- **Champions** - They may often initiate the buying process. They also own the problem that the buyer collective is trying to solve and take the lead in the process. Champions are the most important stakeholder.
- **Decision-makers** - The second-most important stakeholder is the decision-maker. This person usually controls the budget but may also be the champion's boss or at least a senior executive responsible for the outcomes of the decision.
- **Influencers** - There are many influencers, and they are typically involved throughout the process. They provide opinions and requirements, and they can sway which way the champion leads the process.

You need to define the buyer collective for each of your ICPs. This could mean you have two or three buyer collectives, each with champions, decision-makers, and influencers.

Once you have defined the buyer collective, the next step is to create personas for members of the multiple buyer collectives.

How many personas should you create? If you have two ICPs, and each has five members in its buyer collective, you could create ten personas. In our view, ten is unmanageable. We feel you should limit yourself to four personas, especially at first. This will include all the champions and possibly one or two key influencers. We recommend four, as using more can be very cumbersome and hard to do well. It is easy to expand on that number later.

The Buyer Journey Process

There has been some debate about the value of personas and brings up a good question. In our view, there is little point in creating beautifully designed, highly researched personas that sit on the shelf. If they are not actively used in your sales and marketing activities, why bother?

We go through the hard work of creating personas because they define the buyer journey in a useful and compelling way. To us, the buyer journey is the single, most important activity in defining your ABM strategy. It serves as the foundation for an effective engagement plan.

There are five steps in defining a buyer's journey:

1. **Create the buyer persona** - This is where you create a persona that represents your buyer collective stakeholder.
2. **Define their issues and questions** - In this step, you brainstorm a list of questions and issues they have as they go through their buying process.

3. **Determine what information they need** - Here, you list the types of information and content they found useful at each step of the journey.

4. **Identify what they search for** - As the buyer is actively searching for information throughout the buying process, here you develop an initial list of search terms and intent topics you believe the buyer will use.

5. **Define their trusted sources of information** - Lastly, you create a list of content and information sources the buyer will go to for ideas, insight, and inspiration.

We believe this process should be collaborative and can be best executed as a workshop with your organization's subject matter experts, who have real experience and insight about the buyers. It should include sales, marketing, and customer representatives.

If you can afford the time and investment, these steps should be informed by customer insight interviews.

Step 1 - Create the Buyer Persona

Your aim at this juncture is to create a persona that is as real and credible as possible. You are trying to fashion an artifact that will be used to train people in understanding the buyer. It can also be used to gain alignment when discussing issues related to target audiences.

Here is an example of a persona:

CIO/CTO John Davies of XYX Corp	Goals	Needs	Key Issues
• BSc in Computer Science from University of Delaware • MBA from University of Denver • 20 years' experience in IT • Joined XYZ Corp as CIO two years ago • Oversees the organization's technology-related strategies and initiatives. He's responsible for managing digital transformation and the championing agile practices throughout the company • Reports to COO • Manages a team of thirty	• IT operations to meet regulatory requirements - Set direction and vision for privacy compliance program -ensuring compliance with legal, ethical, regulatory, accreditation, licensing, certification requirements • Company data and technical infrastructure is supported, maintained and safeguarded	• Keeping mission-critical infrastructure that keeps organization running from being slow or go down • Unreliable data network required for sharing large data files across multiple locations • Insufficient backup, recovery, and failover solution • Inadequate patient information security • Hardware and software evaluations • Managing multiple vendors • HIPAA Risk Analysis / Risk Assessment - compliance monitoring, oversight, and reporting • Ensure great user experience for call center staff	• XYZ works with mid-size financial firms with call centers to implement enterprise-level HIT, that is more reliable and secure than traditional systems • Help centers implement business continuity and contingency systems to run critical applications like billing, appointment scheduling and account management • We ensure compliant infrastructure • 24/7/365 dedicated support team

Go to at https://learn.totalcustomergrowth.com
to download this example.

As you can see, a typical persona includes:

- Name
- Title
- Where they work
- Their responsibilities
- Their role in the buying process

The latter point is based on customer insight gleaned from the team's collective expertise and possibly customer research.

It helps to find a real buyer on LinkedIn and use their information to populate the framework.

Step 2 - Define Their Issues and Questions

Now, we get into the most important step in this process—defining what is important to them and what they need to get answers to as they go through their buying process.

We break this into four stages that the buyer collective goes through. Three of these are referenced in Chapter 1:

1. **Problem definition** - The buyer collective is trying to frame the problem they are trying to solve as specifically as possible. This is part of intent identification.
2. **Solution definition** - Once they have agreed on the problem they are solving, the buyer collective evaluates different types

of solutions. They need a lot of help here. This is part of intent identification and engagement.

3. **Vendor evaluation** - They compare different options that address the solution they seek to implement. This is part of engagement.

4. **Decision-making** - Lastly, the buyer collective needs to align and decide which vendor to appoint. This is the convert phase.

Note: Traditionally, the steps used in this process are awareness > consideration > interest > decision.

We prefer to use our own approach, which focuses on how the persona buys rather than how you want to move them through your funnel.

In this step, you brainstorm the questions and issues you think the persona is trying to get answers to. Again, base this on the best facts you have, but try to be disciplined about what the buyer is really looking for rather than what you *hope* they are looking for.

One of the most important topics is what triggers them to start investigating the problem. What is going on in their business that bubbled this problem up to the top? What has made this a priority? Is there a compelling event that kicked things off?

Here is what this might look like:

INTENT IDENTIFICATION	ENGAGE		CONVERT
Problem Definition	**Solution Definition**	**Vendor Evaluation**	**Decision**
<u>Infrastructure Triggers:</u> • **Moving offices** • **How do we manage data more efficiently?** • **My data servers are getting old** • Network is slow. • Voice calls are dropping. • No disaster recovery • What happens when circuit fails? • Auto-failover? • Back-up circuit **<u>Other Challenges</u>** • Staff turnover is a big problem. "We can't find anyone!" • "We've been hacked!" • **"Business Continuity"** • **Minimize cybersecurity threats** • Providing better end user support	<u>Decision Flow</u> 1. **Can my ERP do this?** 2. **What do I do if my ERP can't do this?** 3. **What can my existing vendors resolve?** 4. **What are my peers doing?** 5. What will our partners require that we use? **<u>Topics they will research.</u>** • What should I outsource? • What are new options with customer onboarding and account management? • What are my options to improve my infrastructure? • **We are moving. What do we do?** • **What are ways to improve internal user support?**	<u>Research Topics</u> 1. What other customers do you have? 2. What other vendors do this? 3. Trade shows for research 4. How do I create a RFP for this? **<u>Vendor Topics</u>** 1. How long have they been in business? 2. How are you compliant? 3. Where are you located? Can you serve our needs locally? 4. How will your solution integrate with our ERP? 5. Can we have relationship with these guys?	Speak with references Pricing: Often go with lowest bid Do they like you? Can we trust the to be there for us?

You will see in the next chapter how this exercise drives your content strategy.

Step 3 - Determine What Information They Need

The next step is to brainstorm the types of information they need, which will be especially helpful when you get to the next phase and start engagement planning.

If you put yourself in the champion's shoes, think about the type of information that will help them as they work with the rest of the buyer collective. Think beyond the content you can create. While they might find that useful, they also look for information outside your domain. This could include:

- Market research
- Analysts' reports
- Articles by key opinion leaders
- Conference presentations
- The opinions of people in their network
- Buying guides
- RFP frameworks
- Customer reviews
- Implementation guides

Step 4 - Identify What They Search For

Do not forget that for most of the buyer journey, the champion and influencers will not be on your website or speaking with your sales-people. They search and browse the internet for information that helps them long before they engage with you.

Two key questions to answer in creating the buyer journey:

- What search terms and key phrases will they use as they research?
- What intent topics are available and relevant to the buyer journey you are working on?

We will not spend a lot of time on the first question. We could write a whole book on search strategy. The key is to build your search strategy around the personas.

We expand on intent data in Chapter 3. The vendors of third-party data can provide you with the topics they cover.

Here is what the output of steps 3 and 4 look like.

Go to https://learn.totalcustomergrowth.com
to download this example.

INTENT IDENTIFICATION	ENGAGE		CONVERT
Problem Definition	Solution Definition	Vendor Evaluation	Decision
Intent Topics: • Digital Banking • Financial IT • Open Banking	Intent Topics: • Banking as a Service (BaaS) • Digital Monitoring Products (DMP) • Remote Teller	Intent Topics: • Cap Gemini (CAP) • Boston Consulting Group • Thomson Reuters Checkpoint	
Sources of Trust: • Associations and Trade Shows • Local IT Groups Fintech Futures	Sources of Trust: • Peers • Associations and Trade Shows: • Local IT Groups • LinkedIn Groups • LinkedIn is important Fintech Weekly • Banking Technology	Sources of Trust: • Capterra • G2 • Analysts	Sources of Trust: • Vendor customers • Analysts
Types of Information: • Trend reports • Stories about orgs like us and what result they got • Financial analysis (ROI) • Latest best practice	Types of Information: • Case Studies • How to's • Buyer guides • Solution definitions • Top 5 things to consider	Types of Information: • Comparison Matrix • RFP Template • Success Stories and testimonials • Cost/Pricing guide • ROI • Demo's • Integration Guide • Milestones • Implementation guide • Device guide	Types of Information: • References • SSOC2 Certification

Step 5 - Define Their Trusted Sources of Information

The last step is also very helpful as you plan how to engage the buyers. It defines what sources they trust as they search for information to help them in their quest to find the best solution.

As you can see in the buyer journey example above, this includes trade shows, conferences, and various types of publications.

Once you have conducted the workshop to create the buyer journey, document it as a shareable asset and use it as a training tool for sales, marketing, and customer success.

We suggest that you reevaluate these annually at a minimum. What have you learned? What new insights have been gathered? What new additions to the team have new perspectives? All this can help you refine these personas as part of your planning process.

● ● ●

Your next steps will be to create content and campaigns that address the issues surfaced in the buyer journeys. Before we dive into that, there are some important ABM-specific concepts that need to be explained. In the next chapter, we review the types of ABM campaigns to consider and why personalization should be a key part of your plans.

Go to https://learn.totalcustomergrowth.com to access resources for this chapter including a Buyer Journey Template.

CHAPTER 6

Campaign Strategies and Personalization

What You Will Learn in This Chapter

- Why personalization is such an important aspect of ABM and why it works
- What the three types of an ABM campaign are
- How to get started and then scale these personalized campaign approaches
- Some examples of ABM campaigns
- How to evolve into a fully ABM-enabled campaign model

One of the fundamental things that makes ABM different is personalization. In this chapter, we review why personalization is important, the different ways to use it, and how to create ABM and ABX campaigns using personalized approaches. We also review how implementing ABM will change your marketing department's operations.

In terms of the Total Customer Growth journey, this chapter is primarily related to the Identify Intent and Engage stages. However, this will also help in Convert and Grow.

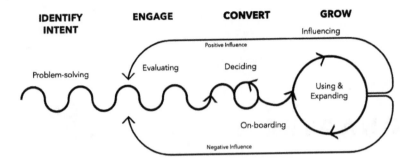

Why Personalization Matters

ABM and ABX are about dedicating your marketing resources more precisely to fewer people. they are the opposite of a mass approach. ABM campaigns are based on the insights you have about the accounts you are targeting and what you know about the buying behavior of personas in each account's buyer group.

The availability of different types of intent and behavioral data means you are missing a big opportunity if you do not use them to personalize your marketing. And when you target ABX programs at existing customers, you risk alienating them by not showing them that you know them.

Personalization also matters because it works. According to McKinsey, the value of getting personalization right (and the cost of getting it wrong) is multiplying. They report that 76% of purchasers are more likely to buy from brands that personalize, and 78% are more likely to recommend your brand to others if you personalize (November 2021). In B2B markets, personalization is becoming table stakes.

According to Forrester, personalization continues to be a priority for B2B marketing leaders, with 52% planning to increase spending on content marketing and personalization technology to get it right (Forrester Business Technographics® Marketing Survey, 2020).

The building blocks of a personalization strategy connect audience, content, and delivery. In Forrester's opinion, this connection is about three things:

- **Assess the audience** - First, define target segments and their attributes according to the type of personalization desired for the tactic, focusing on job role, market segment, and behavioral characteristics.

- **Map and tag content** - Content requirements are driven by the type of personalization being targeted, including personas involved, buying stage, knowledge requirements, and content formats. Ensure content is tagged properly to increase findability, automate activation, and contribute to audience intelligence.

- **Drive delivery with data** - The data available or desired for each audience segment and activation channel fuels targeting, delivery, messaging treatment, and optimization.

Personalization is ultimately about getting the right content in front of the right customer and buying persona so that it resonates and provides compelling value.

Here are a few examples of personalization in action:

- **Email** - When you recognize that a buyer is showing intent signals, you can drop them into email campaign sequences tailored to the topics they are showing intent for and their stage in the buying cycle.

- **Dynamic ad personalization** - Tools like Folloze allow you to brand digital ads with messages and branding tailored to a specific account, so ads are customized and reflect their stage in the buyer journey.

- **Content personalization** - Personalization tools allow you to curate content and brand the page for a specific prospect. The content can be adjusted to the customer's stage in the buying cycle. If the buying signals suggest they are early in the process, the content may be more general and educational. Later in the buying cycle will be the right time to present comparisons versus competitors.

- **Personal URLs (PURLs)** - These allow you to personalize the web URL to the person you are emailing—for example, healthlaunchpad.com/your.name. When recipients visit the web page, they are greeted with a personalized welcome. Content is curated to their needs.

The Three ABM Campaign Types

In simple terms, there are three types of campaigns to consider:

- **1:1, or strategic ABM** – Use this approach when targeting fewer than 50 accounts. Typically, this involves deep account research, highly tailored marketing, and a focus on relationship development.

- **1:Few, or segment ABM** - Use when you target 50 to 200 accounts and can cluster accounts based on commonalities, such as market segment, common need, or potential fit with a specific offering you are testing.

- **1:Many, or ABM at scale** - This one is for firms trying to apply ABM principles to reach thousands of accounts. It is highly data driven and uses intent data and often an orchestration platform to determine which accounts are in-market and target them with personalized messages.

Here are some examples:

1:1 ABM Approach

Company A has long-term agreements with around 50 major manufacturers. It is looking for ways to cross-sell additional services. The company ran a pilot using intent data to identify who was in the market for these additional services. By switching on intent data, they immediately identified that one of their largest customers was showing high interest in this additional service. This customer was unaware that Company A offered this service. The account manager identified the right person for the customer to speak with. After hearing about Company A's capabilities, the customer agreed to add them to their RFP.

Company A's SDR team implemented this technique across 25 major accounts and integrated intent data from ZoomInfo into Salesforce. The SDRs started their daily prospecting routines by focusing on the high-intent accounts.

1:Few ABM Approach

This involves targeting clusters of prospects who have something in common. For example, Company B has a technology-enabled service that is especially useful to customers that use a certain enterprise resource planning (ERP) platform. The company determined that new customers that had most recently adopted this ERP platform had a higher need for Company B's solution.

Company B identified that customers with this ERP platform typically realized this issue was problematic only a year after switching.

Company B developed an ABM campaign targeting about 200 accounts known to have switched ERP platforms in the last three years. It also compiled a list of about 1,000 contacts across these accounts, representing the typical buyer collective. These accounts were targeted with LinkedIn and email sequences using messages, content, and other tactics tailored to the problems these accounts encountered.

1:Many ABM Approach

This approach is difficult to do at scale without implementing an ABM platform, such as 6sense, Terminus, or Demandbase. You can, however, test out hypotheses about 1:Many ABM in simple ways, such as LinkedIn ads.

For example, Company C ran a multivariate test using LinkedIn ads promoting multiple solutions across 650 accounts.

In the first three weeks, Company C set a baseline by running ads on LinkedIn to a defined buyer collective across the 650 accounts. In weeks four through six, Company C used third-party intent data from ZoomInfo to narrow the TAL to those showing intent. By refining the target to only those with intent signals, ad performance increased. They found that over the three weeks, engagement with these ads increased by 50%.

Scaling Personalized Campaigns

Once you have gotten your feet wet, it is time to start scaling up the way you use ABM. There are several components to successfully executing a scalable personalized campaign model.

- **Content** - You will need a great deal of content, likely significantly more than you currently have in place. This content is necessary because you will need to address more precise needs for more personas across different clusters of accounts at different stages of the buyer journey. Doing so can be intimidating and is one of the main reasons ABM and ABX are considered expensive.

- **Technology** - You can execute ABM campaigns in a limited way with technology you may already have in place, especially if you can access intent data. However, to implement ABM at scale, you will need to adopt an ABM platform (e.g., Demandbase, Triblio, RollWorks, Terminus, or 6sense). In addition, you may want to consider tools that make it easier to personalize ads, landing pages, and content (e.g., Folloze, Uberflip, PathFactory). Personalization tools make it easy to create personalized content, messages, and landing pages, which will need to be well-integrated with your CRM and marketing automation platforms. We dedicate a whole chapter to the types of technology and how to use them later in the book.

- **Alignment and communication** - Unlike traditional B2B marketing, where sales and marketing tend to be siloed, ABM is a team sport. Marketing and sales must be joined at the hip in acquiring new customers. Together, the team looks at intent signals, determines how to address the needs of a cluster of accounts, and runs personalized approaches to improve engagement. In more experienced ABM teams, the SDRs start to take on tasks typically associated with marketing, such as creating personalized landing pages. In an ABX scenario, customer success is a key component of the team. They advocate for customers, pinpoint their needs, and guide them on how to best personalize campaigns.

- **Agility** - ABM works best as a team sport, moving quickly and adapting to buying signals and other buyer behavior. This is how to gain a competitive advantage. If you can act more nimbly than the other guys, you can beat them in winning the customer. We are seeing several organizations adopt Agile marketing as an operating model.

ABM Campaign Examples

Let's look at some examples of real-life ABM campaigns that B2B firms have successfully implemented.

Competitive Switching Program

In this case, a firm wanted to target competitors' customers to entice them to switch. Here are the steps in this type of program.

1. **Identify competitors' accounts** - Through in-depth research, the sales and marketing team identified 250 target accounts that used their number-one competitor's solution.
2. **Set up the campaign** - They then exported the 250 target accounts out of Salesforce and into Terminus and used Terminus to set up a campaign targeting those 250 accounts. This included using Terminus's display network to look for prospects from these competitors. The team selected intent topics that would identify when an account might be looking at alternative solutions.
3. **Personalize messaging** - They designed a series of ads and a landing page that focused on how competitors were switching

to their company. The landing page included copy on why companies were switching, the benefits of the firm's solution, a side-by-side comparison of the two solutions, customer testimonials, and calls to action.

Segment-Based Campaign

In this example, the same firm wanted to segment prospects based on different needs that the firm's various solutions could meet. For example, one segment might be interested in facilities management solutions, another in cybersecurity, another in device management, etc.

1. **Create intent topic clusters** - The first step was to create clusters of intent topics in their Terminus ABM platform for each segment using Bombora's intent data. Each cluster reflected each segment's different needs.

2. **Create different marketing campaigns** - For each segment, they created digital ads and a landing page specifically designed for that need. They set these up as different segment-specific campaigns in their Terminus ABM platform.

3. **Drop prospects into the right sequences** - SDRs tracked to see when an account was showing intent for a specific need segment. When they saw that one of their target accounts was showing intent, they dropped it into the relevant campaign. As a result, relevant contacts from those accounts were exposed to digital ads specific to their need. The targeting was adjusted so that only people with specified titles saw the ads. In addition, the firm used Salesloft to initiate a personalized email sequence to target contacts at these accounts.

1:1 ABM Campaign

In a 1:1 campaign, you dedicate significant resources and energy to a small number of large accounts. It is critical to know as much as you can about each account. Here is an example of the steps in a 1:1 campaign.

1. **Identify and select key accounts** - At another firm, sales and marketing would start each quarter by determining which accounts to target with a 1:1 campaign. Typically, they selected five to ten target accounts per quarter. Before starting the campaign, marketing analyzed each account to determine how to best tailor the program to their needs. This involved monitoring and analyzing the engagement and intent data of each particular account on their website. They looked at which relevant topics these top accounts searched for. They also looked at their own HubSpot data to determine how each of their selected accounts engaged with them.

2. **Create account-branded pages** - Based on their analysis, they created an account-branded landing page for their 1:1 marketing campaign for each of their target accounts, featuring their logo and including a personal welcome message. More importantly, the marketing team custom-curated content for each account based on the interest each account showed intent for. This included relevant blog posts, case studies, guides, and highlighting of the most relevant product offerings. They even tested using a video of their CEO personally welcoming the account. This method created a single place where anyone could read about the value the firm offered and what it could offer that specific organization.

3. **Implement individual prospecting for 1:1 marketing** – Then, the AEs prospected with the account-branded pages to engage individual targets within each account and tracked usage. Often, champions at an engaged account want to own the page and share it across the organization, including up the chain to their executive or C-suite.

Evolving Fully to an ABM Campaign Model

As you execute more ABM campaigns and gain confidence, your marketing team will start to operate in a more ABM-like way. The evolution to your marketing department using ABM as its primary strategy will feel natural. Hopefully, you will feel more in control of how effective your marketing is and how much better sales and marketing are operating together.

As a marketer, there are some critical skills you will need to master:

- **Seeing the signals** - As an ABM marketer, you have access to data that empowers you to see signals no one else can. For example, you may see a big wave of interest in a particular topic. By monitoring which content prospects are engaging with on your website and social media channels, looking at patterns in a broad set of intent topics, and monitoring conversations in social media, you can identify changes in the market that will affect your company before the impact hits.

- **Organizing by buyer stage** - As we reviewed in the prior chapter, it is especially important in ABM to understand and organize your marketing around the buyer life cycle. Platforms like 6sense make this easy. You can analyze which accounts are at which stage based on the intent topics they are searching for. You can set up campaigns by buyer stage. This includes creating ad campaigns designed to each buyer stage that will move the buyer from stage to stage. You need modular content that fits the different stages and can be personalized to in-market accounts. And you need to develop expertise in the different email sequences that work best at the different stages of the buyer journey.

- **Collaborating** - At the risk of beating a dead horse, alignment between sales and marketing is the most critical factor in ABM success. You can foster that alignment by facilitating a more collaborative environment and setting up routine check-ins between sales and marketing. This is where your ability to see the signals and organize by buyer stage becomes key. In these meetings, you should bring in the insights you are seeing—especially the visibility of what is happening on an account-by-account basis. Together, marketing and sales should determine the next best action, what you are going to do this coming week, and what is important over the long term.

- **Being Agile** - Rigid, siloed structures get in the way of implementing ABM. To that end, we are seeing more marketing departments adopt an Agile methodology as their operating model. This adoption also means that you will be able to respond faster to changes in buyer behavior and new account insights from your pipeline. Build the notion of test and learn into your plan. It is important to create the space to try new things and keep learning what works and what does not.

● ● ●

In the next chapter, we take the step into planning. Now that you have a buyer journey mapped out and understand the concepts, it is time to start planning how you will engage buyers and what content you will use.

Are you ready to get planning?

Go to https://learn.totalcustomergrowth.com to access resources for this chapter including the Total Customer Growth Planning Framework.

CHAPTER 7

Engagement and Content Planning

What You Will Learn in This Chapter

- How to decide what type of ABM campaign to use
- How to use the buyer journey to plan your campaign
- What the engagement planning framework is and how to use it
- How to plan what content to create using the buyer journey
- How to translate it all into a marketing plan

Similar to the prior chapter, in terms of the Total Customer Growth journey, this chapter is primarily related to the Identify Intent and Engage stages. However, this information will also help in Convert and Grow.

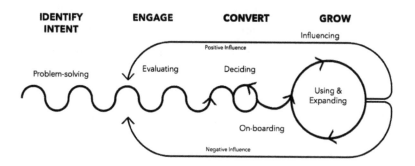

What Types of ABM Campaign to Employ

The first decision is what types of ABM campaigns you will use. It is very common to use more than one.

The size of the TAL and how you segment it will determine your approach. For example:

- If you are targeting fewer than 50 large accounts, you will want to use a 1:1 campaign.
- If you have very large TAL and have segmented it into clusters of 50 to 200 accounts based on commonalities, such as size of organization, common need, and geography, you will want to use a 1:Few segment-based campaign.
- If you are targeting more than 200 accounts and are not able to segment this further, you will want to employ a 1:Many ABM campaign.

Being Buyer Journey driven

The next level of planning is about how you use the buyer journey to create a detailed plan to engage buyers throughout their journey, using a variety of tactics and content tailored to the buyers.

Let's drill down on this a bit by buyer journey stage.

During the Problem Definition stage, the buyers do their initial research online, tapping into their social network and trusted peers for insights and information. As a marketer, your role at this stage is to educate them, make them aware, and start to engage with them.

As they move into Solution Definition, they continue to use the web and their social network, both online and in person, to research and gain ideas and insights. In addition to educating and engaging the buyers, your role at this point is to start making connections either through social media channels or by capturing information about the buyers as they engage with you.

At some point, they start Vendor Evaluation and need help by presenting findings and recommendations to the buyer committee. Your role is to market harder to get them to contact your company.

Finally, they will be Deciding. They will be evaluating you (hopefully) and will want validation that you would be a good choice. Ultimately, they will make a decision. Your role is to make the difference between you and your competitors clear. And as you move to close the deal, you will need to assure them that they are making the right decision. This means convincing the buyer collective that you will deliver on the goals and outcomes they are looking for. In particular, you will need to make the champion feel confident that selecting you is going to make them look good when the company achieves the results it needs.

The Engagement Planning Framework

Below is the engagement planning framework. You will want to create one for each campaign you are planning. It is designed to help you map out a tactical plan that tracks across the buyer journey. For illustration, we show a completed plan.

Stage	INTENT	ENGAGE	CONVERT
Objective	Educate and Engage the Buyer Collective	Solution Sell/ Convert Champions	Close deal
Owned	<ul><li>Educational Content</li><li>Email marketing</li><li>Prospecting using intent data focused on Buyer Collectives within TAL</li><li>Landing Pages</li><li>(Branded if possible)</li><li>LinkedIn Prospecting sequences</li></ul>	<ul><li>Solution-oriented content</li><li>Comparison sheets</li><li>Case Studies</li><li>Prospecting using intent data focused on Buyer Collectives within TAL</li><li>Sales Aides</li><li>Demo Videos</li></ul>	<ul><li>Implementation Guides</li><li>References</li></ul>
Paid	<ul><li>Intent-targeted LinkedIn Educational Ads</li><li>Paid ad or article</li><li>Syndicated Content</li><li>Association Marketing Programs</li><li>Conferences and trade show presence</li></ul>	<ul><li>LinkedIn Lead-generation Ads</li><li>Retargeting</li><li>Netline Buyer Guide</li><li>Intent Data</li><li>Paid Search</li></ul>	<ul><li>Capterra</li><li>G2</li></ul>

Earned	• Press releases • Byliners • Quotes in articles • Analyst relations • Bloggers • Awards • Speaking engagements • Getting on podcasts		• Success Stories in media
Measurement	Target Account Influence: Views, engagement, leads	Target Account Engagement: : Views, engagement, opportunities	Influenced deal conversion attribution. Closed deals

Register at
https://learn.totalcustomergrowth.com
to download this template.

As you can see, this one-page framework allows you to lay out all the key information you need to create a detailed tactical plan. From left to right, it follows the buyer journey as described above, as well as your objectives at each stage.

For reference, you can include your message (or messages) and the target audience. The tactics are split into:

- **Paid** - Tactics you need to pay a third party to execute (e.g., a trade show or an ad campaign on LinkedIn)
- **Owned** - Tactics and assets you own, such as your website and marketing content
- **Earned** - Marketing and communications tactics that earn you exposure and engagement, such as public relations and analyst relations

Last, we include a section to define the measures you use at each stage.

Completing this framework can be fun. We suggest a workshop where you invite members of your sales and marketing teams, along with subject matter experts in digital marketing, PR, event planning, and social media.

You can brainstorm tactics using the personas and buyer journeys to provide direction and guardrails for your ideas. The sources of trust and intent data topics should provide plenty of inspiration.

Typically, we can address the needs of all personas through a single engagement plan. However, if there are significant differences in the roles and characteristics of some of your personas, you may need to do this exercise multiple times.

As you refine the ideas, look for opportunities to develop test programs. For example, you can test intent data with LinkedIn ads that target a defined account list.

Also look for opportunities to personalize. One tactic we find useful is the use of PURLs, or personalized landing pages. They allow you to target engaged buyers that may be halfway along the buyer journey with content curated for them with a personalized URL.

This whole framework depends on content, so let's review how to use this same approach to develop your content plan.

Buyer-Journey-Driven Content Planning

When it comes to creating effective content, we are big believers in the premise of the book *They Ask, You Answer: A Revolutionary Approach to Inbound Sales, Content Marketing, and Today's Digital Consumer* by Marcus Sheridan. Its basic idea is that buyers are looking for answers to all the questions they have as they go through the buyer journey.

As you saw in the previous chapter, we believe that when you create personas, you should put your greatest effort into the questions the champion personas have at each stage of the journey.

The role of your content is to answer these questions.

Here is the process you will go through to create a content plan or calendar:

1. Define your ICPs, then the personas and generate the list of questions each persona has throughout the buyer journey.
2. Create content topics that answer each question. These content topics will be turned into your content, plan, and editorial calendar.
3. Identify which questions to focus on. You may have generated dozens of questions for each persona. If you have four personas, you may create a list of hundreds of questions. Clearly, it would be overwhelming to create a content plan with 200 pieces of content to answer each of these questions. So, you will need to prioritize which questions to focus on. You may want to narrow it down to the top five questions per persona. In the resource at learn.totalcustomergrowth.com, you can see an example of this in action. It shows a prioritized list that is still long, but significantly shorter than the full list.
4. Get a team back together and start brainstorming ideas on different types of content that could answer these questions. We use a simple framework for this that you can download at learn.totalcustomergrowth.com.
5. Combine topics so you can leverage content across multiple personas. For each topic, create a short abstract describing what each post or long-form video will do.

6. Ensure that you cover the buyer journey effectively. To that end, we recommend a simple content matrix that maps the final content topics against the personas. This ensures that you have all the personas' high-priority questions addressed at each stage of the buyer journey. You can see examples at learn. totalcustomergrowth.com.

Turning This into a Marketing Plan

Now that you have a tactical framework to engage your personas across the buyer journey, you need to turn it into a plan and budget.

We start this by prioritizing what will be done by quarter. There is an example in the online resource center.

Once you have completed this prioritization, we suggest that you create a simple Gantt chart to describe your plan for the upcoming quarter, accompanied by a budget.

●　　●　　●

One of the key questions you will need to think through is what technology you need to implement this. It is so important that we dedicate the whole next chapter to this issue. It is key as you move into executing your campaigns.

> Go to https://learn.totalcustomergrowth.com
> to access resources for this chapter including
> the Engagement Planning template.

PART 2

Executing ABM

What You Will Learn in Part 2

Part 2 is about moving from strategy into action. This will help you put in place some of the key capabilities you will need to execute ABM.

- Chapter 8 is about technologies to consider and when—especially the celebrated ABM platform.
- In Chapter 9, we explain how to turn your SDR team into an ABM engine.
- Chapter 10 helps you develop an effective Total Customer Growth measurement model.

This section primarily focuses on the Identify Intent, Engage, and Convert stages of the Total Customer Growth Model.

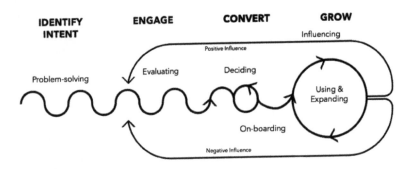

CHAPTER 8

The ABM Technology Platform

What You Will Learn in This Chapter

- What your technology choices are and which types to consider
- Whether you need an ABM platform and when you will need it
- What the characteristics of an ICP are
- What to look for in an ABM platform

In this chapter, we share how technology, like an ABM platform, can help you throughout the entire Total Customer Growth Model and especially in the Identify Intent and Engage stages.

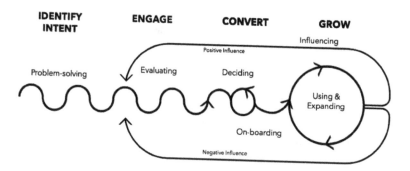

What Technologies to Consider

The choices of marketing technology are overwhelming. At last count, according to Scott Brinker of Chiefmartec.com, there were over 9,000 technology solutions to consider, arrayed across dozens of different categories. This is constantly changing, and it is easy to feel overwhelmed by the available options.

Let's cover the fundamentals. Here are the technologies you will need to consider:

- **Intent data** - This is covered in detail in Chapter 3. It provides buying signals about target accounts. There are two types: first-party intent data (e.g., tools like LeadLander and Leadfeeder, which tell you which accounts are visiting your website) and third-party intent (e.g., Bombora and ZoomInfo's intent data).

- **Contact data** - As intent data typically includes only account-level data, you will need a supplemental source of contact data, such as ZoomInfo, to build a contact list when an account appears on your radar screen.

- **CRM** - You will no doubt have this already. CRM platforms—like Salesforce, HubSpot, and Zoho—are where your sales team works and is usually where accounts and contacts are stored and accessed. As we discuss further on, while ABM campaigns are not managed here, it will be important to create ABM dashboards in your CRM. This is critical to engaging the sales team in your ABM and ABX program. As your SDRs start work in the morning, you want them to look at a dashboard and see which accounts are showing what intent they should focus on. This will help them prioritize who they outreach to. It will show what topics buyers are researching and make it easy to personalize SDR, sales, or customer success activities.

- **Marketing automation** – You may already have this platform in place. Platforms like Pardot, Marketo, and HubSpot enable you to easily run automated marketing campaigns and measure impact. While many of these include more ABM-like capability, this is limited. Often, you can get started with ABM by integrating third-party intent data into your marketing automation system (e.g., Bombora and Eloqua), but you will struggle to scale to an entire ABM and ABX model without an ABM platform.

- **ABM and ABX platforms** - We cover this in detail below. They include software from companies like 6sense, Terminus, Demandbase, and a handful of others. These multifunction platforms allow you to run your ABM program at scale. One of their most important functions is helping you drive better-informed sales and marketing decisions based on customer behavior. They are your ABM program's automated workflow delivery engine, and they are increasingly the ad platform used to run digital display campaigns.

- **Personalization** - These additional tools make it easier to personalize messaging, ad creative, and landing pages dynamically and at scale. They include Folloze, Uberflip, and PathFactory.

- **Sales outreach** - Your sales and SDR team may already use tools like Salesloft and Outreach.io to automate and measure outbound email and social media prospecting programs.

- **Integration tools** - You will need to integrate the tech stack. These platforms are designed to work together, and integration tools like Zapier facilitate this.

- **Project management** - You will want to have a marketing project management solution to track your campaigns, projects, and tasks. This will be key to tracking cross-functional work for creative, content, and social media. Solutions include Tenon, Workfront, Asana, and Monday.com.

Do You Need an ABM Platform?

The answer is, eventually, yes.

Why?

You can do 1:1 ABM without an ABM platform and pilot 1:1, 1:Few, and 1:Many ABM without an ABM platform. However, without an ABM platform, your business impact will be limited. You will not be able to scale your ABM program due to the lack of automation and the manual labor-intensive processes required to perform the work.

You will also miss out on some amazing capabilities that can change how you generate demand for your business.

Let's start with the age-old problem of generating new prospect leads. In a traditional, broad-based approach, you use various tactics to get prospective buyers to put their hands up and indicate some interest in what you do. Typical tactics include conferences, trade show booths, webinars, syndicated content, Google ads, and targeted LinkedIn ad campaigns.

These all work and have their role in an ABM scenario, but they can be hugely wasteful. In the words of John Miller, a longtime ABM executive and chief product officer at Demandbase, this is like fishing with a net versus fishing with a spear.

The challenge is that when a prospect is active in a buyer journey, they engage with you only in the latter stages. If you are lucky, you might be able to identify them early in the process if they download gated content from your website or register for a webinar that you are running. But the fact is that buyers spend most of their time avoiding you.

An ABM platform makes it easier to identify in-market accounts earlier through intent data, monitor the buyer collective at these accounts, and orchestrate more precisely targeted campaigns that are personalized to who they are and what stage they are in on the buyer journey. It gives you the visibility and power to move a buyer through the journey with you. It allows you to at least track them as they move through the buyer journey. That way, when they are ready to talk to a vendor, there is a greater chance that they will talk to you and be better educated about you.

Here are three real-life scenarios of what selling and marketing look like with and without an ABM platform. In this case, it is for a firm selling sophisticated enterprise software with a $1 million+ annual cost.

No ABM Platform and No Intent Data

Prior to starting on its ABM journey, the firm kept missing out on RFPs. Customers did not know this new company even existed due to the number of vendors that had been around for a long time and had stronger brand awareness. As a result, the firm was not included in the initial vendor list up for consideration. This was painful, as buyers evaluated new solutions every 10 to 15 years. If the firm missed a buying cycle, it would likely not see another opportunity with this customer for a decade. It is clear that missing an opportunity that comes along only once a decade had a detrimental impact on the company's success and longevity.

No ABM Platform but Using Intent Data

To get started with ABM, the firm tried third-party intent data from ZoomInfo. In the first few days, one of the SDRs noticed that a target account they had a good relationship with was spiking for a key topic related to one of their solutions. This signaled that the target might be in-market for their solution. The AE reached out to a contact they knew at that company. This contact put the AE in touch with a more appropriate contact. This second person let the AE know they were developing an RFP. This person was unfamiliar with the software firm's solution in this area and decided to include them in the RFP.

With an ABM Platform

The software firm adopted the Terminus platform. As they became more familiar with the benefits of ABM, the SDR and marketing team could pinpoint an account that was in-market. Rather than have the SDRs immediately reach out, they ran a personalized segment-specific campaign to the account. Based on topics this account was spiking for, they changed the messaging to address that interest. As the account moved to the next stage in the buyer journey, they refined the message accordingly. The team's goal was to move the buyers, or at least a champion, to watch a 15-to-30-minute demo walkthrough video of their solution. They knew they had an educated buyer who was interested enough to dedicate 30 minutes to learning the details and value of the solution. At that point, the SDR reached out with a personalized email and phone call. The buyer responded and indicated that his firm was, in fact, interested in their solution. The close rate for these types of deals are significantly higher.

What to Look for in an ABM Platform

When you review the leading ABM platforms from Demandbase, Terminus, 6sense, Triblio, RollWorks, and others, you will see that they have several functions in common. At the end of the day, they help you take the guesswork out of marketing.

Account Intelligence

Account intelligence is the foundation of ABM. Your ABM platform should make it easier to find the right accounts that are in-market for solutions, engage with them, close those deals faster, and measure it all.

Account intelligence will require you to bring together different types of buyer behavior data, including your first-party intent data from your website analytics and third-party intent data. We review intent data in detail in Chapter 3.

Important: Your sources should help you understand which accounts are in-market for your category of products before they raise their hand. Your ABM platform should also help you identify any accounts coming to your website anonymously.

The more sophisticated platforms use artificial intelligence to provide even greater insight about what customers and prospects are interested in. Some also include firmographics, including industry revenue, employee and account location, financials, etc. Check to see if they include account hierarchies with parent and child account mapping.

Some platforms even help you discover new accounts and expand your total addressable market. Their recommendation engines will show you which accounts you should focus on and help you easily add those to your CRM.

Typically, third-party intent data provides only account-level info, so you will need a way to source contact information for target accounts' key buyers. This should include privacy-compliant contact data that that helps you identify and contact decision-makers across the entire buying team, including name, title, role, email, mobile, phone, and social.

To make this actionable, all this account insight must show up in three key places:

- The ABM platform
- Your marketing automation system
- Your CRM

Why? You can use it to run campaigns and enable your sales execs and SDRs to do their work. This is important because you will be more successful when you minimize disruptions and distractions for your sales team.

When you evaluate these platforms, have multiple use cases and scenarios mapped out. That way, when the ABM platform vendor demos, you can have them slice and dice the data to create account lists in ways that are appropriate for your organization.

Account Prioritization and Predictive Analytics

One of the most valuable things you can do with better account intelligence is find and prioritize target accounts. First, you should be able to easily create customer lists and segments for your accounts and the people who are part of the buying process. This process includes choosing from the most common attributes, like company size, revenue, industry, geography, and technologies.

Some ABM platforms include qualification scoring that uncovers your best-fit accounts and allows you to easily rank and segment your total addressable market. Some even include a predictive model that can quantify the chances of an account becoming an opportunity. This will enable you to invest your time in the best opportunities.

Platforms use machine learning to find patterns that precede opportunities (like a spike in intent or engagement), and then automatically and continuously look for similar patterns at other prospective accounts and your current customers. This tactic lets sales teams prioritize outreach on accounts with a higher probability of converting.

It is critical that the ABM platform also be able to track where an account is in its buyer journey. You will implement campaigns in part based on knowing this. The journey stage will be the core of your campaign, allowing you to know what and when to market to an account.

Orchestration and Personalization

ABM campaigns allow you to engage intelligently with your accounts at just the right time and in just the right way, as efficiently as possible. Your role is orchestrating interactions across channels and systems and using targeted advertising and website personalization to attract and engage the right people in the correct accounts.

The dashboard should allow you to create target audience segments. For example, you should be able to take all accounts in the awareness or problem-definition stage and put them on a campaign list, or push all buyer group members engaged with vendor evaluation-oriented marketing content into a direct-mail or gifting campaign.

You will want to sync your account and people list to third-party advertising destinations, like LinkedIn, Facebook, Instagram, and Twitter, so you can orchestrate a multichannel advertising approach.

This way, your ads can update automatically as accounts move through the journey or enter new segments.

Ask the vendor how you can use their platform to orchestrate campaigns across all of these channels:

- Social networks (LinkedIn, Twitter, Facebook)
- Display ads
- Email
- Direct mail
- Video
- In-person events and conferences
- Blogs
- Webinars
- Mobile

Several of these platforms also provide a demand-side advertising platform (DSP) to automatically manage the delivery of ad impressions. Ask vendors how they can maximize your programmatic spending and how they handle brand safety, so ads are served only on a publisher whitelist.

In more advanced campaigns, you should be able to connect to streaming services, like Hulu, Spotify, Disney+, etc., so you can reach buyers with personalized ads wherever they are.

We cover measurement below, but you will want to know how the platform measures ROI and determines a campaign's impact.

Most importantly, you need to understand how each platform handles personalization. How will the platform improve the way your accounts receive a relevant experience when they visit your website, whether driven by an ad or arriving organically? Can it help you personalize the website based on their journey stage and create tailored experiences that will improve conversion?

Improved Sales Conversion

As we covered previously, the account intelligence needs to be at your sales fingertips, right inside CRMs, like Salesforce. Aligning marketing, sales, and customer success is key. Having these groups in the same CRM system they use today and not requiring them to go into another system for ABM will be a key to the program's adoption and success.

Ideally, your ABM platform will automatically populate account info in the CRM with information that will make the sales AE and SDR better informed (e.g., account hierarchies, news alerts, social alerts, and buying intent signals).

This will help your sales team reach out in a more relevant way and make it easier to impress buyers with knowledge about leadership changes, financial results, and other key news that may drive a compelling event.

More importantly, the sales team should have a single view that displays intent signals from third-party intent data and engagement insights, such as website visits, email interactions, etc. Ideally, the ABM platform or your CRM will aggregate email, phone, and in-person communication history. Ask them how the platform empowers the salesperson through better insights. Having a strong revops (revenue operations) or marops (marketing operations) person will be key to success.

Some of the platforms offer web plug-ins so that when salespeople are prospecting on LinkedIn, they get more complete contact details, including email addresses, and direct and mobile phone numbers.

Suffice it to say, the ABM platform should also have customizable alerts for important information, such as highlights on the most engaged accounts with highest pipeline predict scores, top intent, keywords, and key engagement signals from your open opportunities.

Lastly, how can the platform help customer success managers? They should be able to see changes within their accounts and quickly respond to opportunities or threats, such as the loss of a champion, expansion into new markets, rising or falling profits, etc. The platform should also identify cross-sell and upsell opportunities for growth and help you know when a customer might be considering a competitor.

Measurement

The last important capability is how the ABM platform allows you to measure your ABM activities. In Chapter 10, we review ABM measurement in detail. Before that, there are some basic features you need from the ABM platform.

At a basic level, you need to see which accounts are visiting which pages of your website, with account identification and associated demographics. Ideally, this can feed into other platforms you might be using.

You need to show how you are driving demand, how you are driving the right types of traffic, and where your target accounts are coming from. The systems should help you understand the behavior of individual accounts, personas, and buying groups, both at a granular and an aggregate level.

In addition, how does the platform display engagement? You want to see across a buyer journey, measure engagement across your accounts, and track how they move through the buyer journey with conversion rates and velocity metrics to understand where they get stuck.

For advertising campaigns, you need to be able to see where every impression was served, and which ads are most successful. In aggregate, you want to know how programs and campaigns across all your marketing channels are performing.

When considering a platform, always ask how it can help you visualize the success of marketing and sales alignment in moving deals through the pipeline.

• • •

The ABM technology platform will give you an advantage over your competition. Your secret weapon is your SDR team. They are critical to the success of your ABM program. In the next chapter, we dive into why and how.

> Go to https://learn.totalcustomergrowth.com
> to access resources for this chapter
> including an ABM Platform Checklist.

CHAPTER 9

SDRs: ABM's Secret Weapon

What You Will Learn in This Chapter

- Why your demand generators are a linchpin in your ABM campaign
- What life is like for a demand generator with and without ABM and why ABM gives them wings
- How ABM changes how demand generators work and how to introduce it to them

Demand generators have different titles, including business development representatives (BDRs) and sales development representatives (SDRs). For convenience, we refer to anyone whose role is to reach out to prospects to create and nurture opportunities as an SDR.

This chapter relates primarily to identifying intent and engaging prospects in the Total Customer Growth Model.

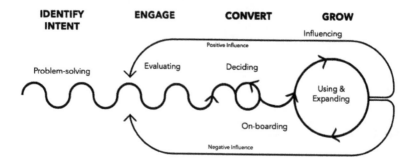

Why SDRs Are So Important in ABM

In B2B marketing, one of marketing's primary roles is to bring prospects to the door of your house. The SDR's role is to open the door and bring them into the house. And sales closes the deal.

The SDRs are even more important in an ABM model. Marketing resources are focused on a narrower set of targets. Each lead is even more likely to be a good fit than in traditional B2B marketing, as the account has been targeted more precisely with personalized content based on interests and current activity. Each lead is even more precious, so getting these leads over the metaphorical threshold is even more important.

Strong alignment between marketing and sales is the key to a successful ABM program. And more importantly, marketing and the SDRs need to work seamlessly together. Arguably, in an organization that values ABM, the SDRs are also part of the marketing organization to ensure complete alignment between the groups.

ABM can transform your SDRs' effectiveness. Let's look at life for SDRs with and without ABM.

Being an SDR Without ABM

What's the day like for SDRs who come into a new SaaS company that is not using ABM?

To start with, they have poorer intelligence in their outreach activities, having only the traditional tools, social media and data sources, like ZoomInfo. The challenge is making the SDRs' jobs easier and making them more successful, in turn increasing those conversions from marketing leads into opportunities and revenue.

Let's start with a story from Ben.

> So, before ABM, what did we do? We had a team of SDRs that defined the target market, or the ideal customers we wanted to call into. They went into Salesloft and began their outreach and targeting. The challenge was that those outreaches, for the most part, were completely cold. They used templated email and phone scripts written by product marketing and polished by marketing writers. But even with those standard talking points, they were sending those messages to a potentially non-engaged buyer. We didn't know if they were in a buying cycle or currently looking for information the SDRs were sending. We didn't know what that buyer was currently using, evaluating, or even interested in. For us, that is as cold as outreach gets. In many cases, they did not even know our company existed.

How ABM Changes the Way an SDR Works

When ABM is effectively implemented, an SDR's life looks very different. It feels like you are delivering automated awareness and automated movement to get buyers interested based on topics they are investigating. Then, you are getting them to convert into a lead. This means SDRs spend more time calling a person who has interest and intent, and they are calling in with real data about that buyer.

For example, your SDR knows what content the prospect is engaging with, what topics they are researching, how long they are on your website, and what competitors they are looking at.

Once you have ABM up and running, your SDRs will be armed with the key intel that will set them up for success in in their outreach. If marketing has done their job well, the buyer will have been targeted with content relevant to them. So, when a phone call or email reaches that potential client, they already know the company exists and why it is reaching out. They have already seen relevant and valuable information that they are researching.

A buyer is more likely to be ready to speak with an SDR, and when an SDR does reach the buyer, the buyer is better informed and more engaged.

SDRs have much more control over the process. It feels like a more deliberate five-step approach:

1. Build targeted brand awareness.
2. Get the best-fit accounts engaged through digital channels.
3. Use intent data to determine who is in-market.
4. Score them based on engagement with your content.
5. When they show enough intent, have your SDRs pursue them using the intent data gathered throughout the process.

But you cannot just turn on an ABM campaign and expect SDRs to start calling tomorrow. You need to warm up the buyers and filter out the accounts not currently in a buying cycle. First, you see intent, then you start to put ads in front of them for an entire month. As the intent increases and there is more interest, your SDRs should follow up. And you will need to cycle through topics and segmentations to engage unresponsive target accounts.

Your objective is to make sure you have enough right accounts with the right information at the right time so that when your SDRs are outreaching, they have an improved hit rate.

SDRs are typically compensated based on their ability to create new customer meetings, generate opportunities, and produce a sales pipeline. By introducing ABM to your SDRs, you are directly and positively affecting their ability to make more commission and increase the company's bottom-line revenue.

A Quick Way to Introduce ABM to Your SDRs

One of the simplest uses of intent data is providing in-market reports to your sales team, especially SDRs. You can do this by integrating the source of intent data with your CRM. Doing this becomes a critical dashboard for the SDRs. A well-designed dashboard combines intent surge data with engagement on the company's website. It creates a spike heat signal that indicates which companies are most actively in-market and engaging with them.

In a project with a client, we used ZoomInfo intent data and saw positive results within a week. Their SDR team was researching current customer intent for a relatively new service they were offering (remote patient monitoring, or RPM). The head of the SDR team saw that a very large current customer was showing intent for RPM but had not purchased it from them. She alerted the account team, and within a few days, they reached the right person at the prospective customer, who said they were about to start an RFP process and would include the client.

• • •

So, you have a well-defined ABM strategy. You have developed a thoughtful buyer journey and created content to engage the champions. You have a tactical plan to test various ABM approaches, and your SDRs are primed and ready to go. Now, the really hard task arrives: measurement. This is the toughest challenge with ABM. In the next chapter, we provide you with a measurement framework and a game plan to develop a measurement model that works for you.

How will you know if this has worked?

Go to https://learn.totalcustomergrowth.com to access resources for this chapter including an interview with Ben Person on how to boost your SDR productivity with intent data.

CHAPTER 10

Measurement Matters

What You Will Learn in This Chapter

- Why ABM requires a different way of measuring effectiveness
- How the ABM measurement framework works
- What revenue, marketing, and campaign performance are and how to measure them
- How to create a Total Customer Growth dashboard
- How to evolve your measurement model over time

This chapter is important throughout the entire Total Customer Growth Model.

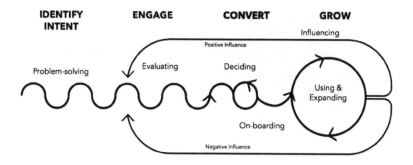

As you are starting or already running your ABM program, one of the keys to success, just like with any other campaign, is ensuring you can accurately measure the results. You cannot turn ABM on and *hope* it works. Hope is not a strategy. Marketers need to look at key measures to ensure the work and the efforts they are putting into their ABM program are providing the results they expected in returning an investment in the program.

How do you go about measuring the impact of ABM? Tracking and measuring ROI remains the leading challenge for ABM practitioners.

Part of the challenge is linked to the large amount of information and data involved. We frequently cannot see the forest for the trees. The other challenge is that in ABM, you need to change how you measure marketing. Traditional marketing key performance indicators (KPIs) are not adequate.

The keys in measuring ABM are sales measures, marketing measures, and campaign measures. Ultimately, we have to look at all three as we track ABX performance.

ABM Measurement Framework

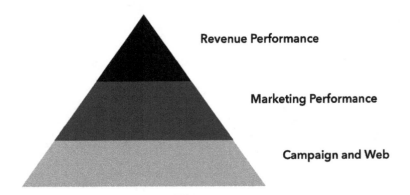

Revenue Performance

Marketing Performance

Campaign and Web

This ABM measurement framework was developed by Demandbase and focuses on measuring performance at three levels.

At the top of the pyramid is revenue performance measurement.

The second level is marketing performance measurement and how it connects to revenue performance.

At the bottom are all the marketing campaigns and web performance measurements.

Under each, there are different key performance indicators.

Revenue Performance Measurement

These are the key strategic measures for revenue performance. If you have a good handle on these three KPIs, you will be better able to forecast revenue. In ABM, it is really important that sales be fully on board with having measurements related to sales activities. So, as you apply ABM to your selling motion, you will need to know how it influences and affects a salesperson's ability to close and win net new revenue.

The next one is your sales cycle, and ABM is not just about finding deals, sourcing them, and getting them in the pipeline. It is also about how you accelerate deals once they are in the pipeline. Salespeople want to find ways to increase the velocity of a selling motion.

Ben's Story

In my prior role, an average sale for a new account could have taken as long as eight to nine months. In some cases, it could take over a year to win a new customer. As a marketer, I had the opportunity to help accelerate opportunities. But as part of that measurement process, I needed to track the average deal cycle times by measuring the actual time from the creation of that opportunity to close with or without ABM running. I needed to know if and how much ABM was impacting the velocity of sales cycles.

By measuring the before ABM and after ABM, I was able to see how applying ABM and producing the right information during an active deal could both grow the size of the opportunity and increase the probability of winning.

I will give you a real-world example: I started to put information in front of a buyer through digital ads and personalized landing pages that allowed me to avoid proof of concept with a customer. I gave them content, and they were able to have an in-depth look at the product demos and product videos, and self-serve on their own time. Additionally, I put customer case studies in front of a buyer during the sales process and avoided another customer reference call. I can do these things as a marketer running an ABM program. I can accelerate a deal cycle because I can avoid major long poles in a selling process. Therefore, you are going to want to measure average deal cycle time in the sales process.

Pipeline velocity is another critical factor. This is not just the overall sales cycle, but measuring each step along that sales journey and how long it takes to move through each step in the selling motion.

Think of your sales approach as a tent. It is important to understand where the long poles are in the process. Is the contracting process the long pole? Is the proof of concept the long pole? Finding where those extended sales areas are and seeing if you can apply ABM to those long poles is important in accelerating deal cycles and driving pipeline velocity. There are many tools you can apply on top of your CRM to measure deal velocity, stage by stage. An example of a deal-velocity tracking tool is Full Circle Insights. It allows you to track the movement of deals through each stage and how long deals stay within each stage. This information allows you to see where you could improve deal velocity and what the impact might be on the average cycle time to close. This can be a way to measure deal cycle times before and after ABM to determine what, if any, impact it may have on deal velocity.

The last factor for sales is your overall deal close rate.

Has your overall deal close rate increased as part of your ABM program? Can you tell how your close rate has changed since implementing ABM? Is that close rate going up? Because now you are allowing more people to get involved in the sales process, putting additional content in front of your buyer, and proving that you are the right solution.

Those sales measures are going to be important when it comes to showing the sales team what marketing can deliver as part of an ABM program. And sales will be all in if you can make a deal larger, decrease their cycle time, enable the pipeline to move faster, and help them win deals faster.

As you develop your measurement framework, here are the three key revenue KPIs.

Deal Close Rates

This is the percentage of deals that close. In other words, what is your hit rate? We recommend measuring the ratio from the qualified opportunity to deal close.

Average Deal Size

In prior roles, we paid a lot of attention to this, as it was the main growth driver. Given how long sales cycles are in certain industries, like government or health care, you may be more successful in impacting this KPI than others.

Salespeople want to increase the average deal size. If a salesperson is pursuing an account, one of the greatest things ABM can do is help them find other products and other lines of business that a prospect could also buy.

Intent data can enable you to identify additional lines of business, cross-sell additional products, and drive up the average deal size, deal by deal. Salespeople receive commissions based on deal size, so finding more revenue in existing customers can drive up their compensation.

Funnel Velocity

This may be the single most important metric. In the words of a former colleague, Matt Pickens, a sales leader in the health care world:

> To get someplace on time, you need to know how fast you are traveling. To hit a sales goal, you need to know how fast you are selling (and how fast your buyers are buying). Speed of selling is also known as sales velocity, which is among the most useful and least understood sales metrics. For any B2B organization looking to achieve greater results, sales velocity offers a simple, yet powerful, framework to accelerate performance.

ABM Measurement

As you implement an ABM program, you put ads in front of prospects, and they engage with those ads. They read your content and learn more about your company. From a marketing standpoint, you need to measure the influence marketing is having on targeted accounts.

You also want to know how much net new pipeline you can influence. You should aim to influence most of the pipeline through ABM, as any new sales opportunity will have been exposed to your campaign.

You can measure many things, such as content engagement rates. How much of your content is being consumed, and how is this impacting the pipeline? How long are people spending time on that content?

Another measure is influence on your existing pipeline. If an opportunity is already in the pipeline, you should be using ABM campaigns to influence close rates and sales cycle duration.

You also need to track marketing's impact on your SDR team. For example, you should track when and how SDRs opened an opportunity, auto-flag when they used intent data to outreach to that account, see content that account has viewed, and know what topics are relevant to them. You want to be able to credit ABM for allowing an SDR to work smarter when they targeted a customer based on intent data.

Here are some specific ABM marketing KPIs to focus on.

TAL Engagement

This involves assessing the extent to which the companies in your TAL engage with your company. The more the engagement or the higher the frequency of engagement, the higher the marketing performance impact.

Pipeline: Percentage of Sales Accounted for by Your TAL

Evaluate the overall percentage of pipeline sales directly linked to your TAL. This ABM measurement will help you evaluate if your TAL is effective for your marketing campaigns.

TAL Website-Engagement Level

This requires you to analyze how many prospects on your TAL have actively engaged on your website, and it may include a wide range of metrics, such as what they are searching for, the links they click, and how long they spend on pages. It also includes how often they return and more.

Total Conversion Rate

While the level of website engagement is critical, the other key measurable marketing metric is your TAL's conversion rate. The higher the conversion rate, the higher your ABM marketing performance.

Influence as an Alternative to Attribution

Attribution is trying to understand a combination of unique events that can influence your target accounts to act. But measuring attribution is very difficult and often inaccurate. Influence may be a better alternative. You can develop influence measures by shifting your analysis to look at engagement in your content and social media channels.

Customer Retention and Upsell

To what extent is your ABM strategy influencing current customers to upgrade their current solutions or purchase more products or services from you?

Cost Per Opportunity

Basically, this measures the cost of getting a new customer.

Campaign and Web Measures

When it comes to campaign measurements, you want to look at ROI. For example, one month into a campaign, how much did you spend on digital ads, and how much pipeline has that generated?

In longer deal cycles, you will want to look at it over a longer period. As the deal reaches closure, look back to last year and review the numbers so you can say, "We ran these campaigns, and here is how much revenue we actually produced."

We often focus just on basic metrics, like web traffic per month, page views, downloads, etc. In fact, these are the building blocks, and they are how you get to marketing measures.

Examples of these measures:

- Cost per lead
- Conversion rate
- Incremental sales, among others

Web performance

This includes but is not limited to the following:

- Total web visits from your TAL
- Bounce rate
- Average time a target customer spends on a page
- New visitors

Dashboards

As you develop dashboards, you can kill two birds with one stone:

- Track your KPIs
- Provide your sales, marketing, and SDR team with a central place to do their work

This means that while you may need an ABM platform to run ABM programs, much of the sales and measurement activity happens in your CRM.

You want to create a single place where your sales teams and SDRs can review first-party data on all their accounts. They want to review items, like who is on your website or social media accounts. You want them to see high-intent accounts that are in a buying cycle right now and spiking in particular topic areas.

You also want to see medium-intent accounts and low-intent accounts that you can nurture and convert into high-intent accounts. A system that works like this steers the SDRs and sales teams to spend their time wisely rather than guessing where those accounts are in their buying process.

Creating Dashboards

It is important to focus on not impacting sales and SDR selling behavior when it comes to their standard operating procedures. So, when it comes to standing up a new ABM dashboard, you will want this to reside in the same CRM that sales and SDRs are already using in their daily selling routines. These dashboards also need to have an easy-to-follow flow for prioritizing accounts they should focus on. They should include both first-party and third-party intent data if possible.

For example, here are some items to include on your ABM dashboard:

- Accounts engaging with your content (first-party data)
- High-intent accounts (not yet engaged with)
- Medium-intent accounts (not yet engaged with)
- Low-intent accounts (not yet engaged with)
- Existing accounts showing intent (cross-sell opportunities for products they do not yet have)

Ideally, as accounts are engaged with, they should automatically fall off this dashboard so that sales and SDRs see only accounts they have not reached out to or created an opportunity for. This way, as sales and SDRs leverage this dashboard each week, they see only new accounts they have not reached out to. Depending on your objectives, you may choose to not have them drop off, but consider that process as part of your dashboard setup.

How to Evolve Your Total Customer Growth Measurement Model

If you are struggling to develop your measurement model, you are in good company. This is consistently a top issue that executives struggle with in ABM. Creating a reliable, forecastable ABM measurement model that everybody buys into may take one to two years.

However, once it is in place, ABM will be accepted as *the* way your company markets and sells. Getting there will take support from leadership and strong collaboration between sales and marketing.

Here are steps you can take to move toward your ideal ABM measurement model:

1. Set Initial ABM KPIs

When you start creating a mix of web, campaign, and ABM marketing measures, pick ones that are easy to monitor and do not require a significant leap of faith from your colleagues. These will be more focused on measuring the effectiveness of individual ABM campaigns and include:

- Conversion rates
- Target account engagement
- Account penetration
- Account influence

2. Set Next-Level Measures

As your ABM program evolves and begins to expand, upgrade the KPIs you measure to include more sophisticated metrics that show how your ABM program is affecting the pipeline overall. For example:

- Pipeline influenced by ABM
- Cost-per-opportunity ABM versus non-ABM
- Percentage of opportunities from your TAL

3. Set Long-Term KPIs

The goal is to develop KPIs that allow you to measure the impact of ABM on key sales attributes. These include:

- Close-rates ABM versus non-ABM
- Average-deal-value ABM vs non-ABM
- Funnel velocity
- Closed-revenue ABM versus non-ABM

● ● ●

We have now covered all the fundamentals of ABM. In Part 3, we look beyond ABM and customer acquisition to explore ABX—the other half of the Total Customer Growth Model.

Let's dive into ABX

> Go to https://learn.totalcustomergrowth.com
> to access resources for this chapter including
> an ABM Measurement Checklist.

PART 3

ABM to ABX

What We Will Cover in Part 3

In Part 1, we focus on ABM marketing's role in identifying and winning new customers. And in Part 2, we explain the key capabilities you need to scale ABM. In Part 3, we shift to ABX as a more holistic approach to growing profitable customer relationships. Together, they create a Total Customer Growth Model.

- In Chapter 11, we help you understand ABX and why it should be a priority.
- Chapter 12 covers the all-important topic of account insight, what it is, and how to get it.
- In Chapter 13, we cover many ways you can turn this insight into growth programs.

In this section, we focus on the Grow stage of the Total Customer Growth Model.

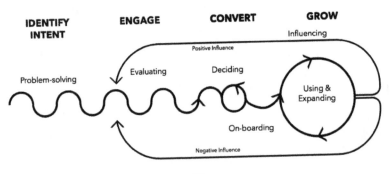

CHAPTER 11

Envisioning ABX and Total
Customer Growth

What You Will Learn in This Chapter

- How you will need to operate differently to be successful in implementing ABX and Total Customer Growth
- How the role of marketing changes with ABX and Total Customer Growth
- The importance of customer life-cycle thinking
- Why marketing needs to take the lead in creating a collaborative environment
- What the keys to success are in moving from ABM to ABX and Total Customer Growth

As we state in Chapter 1, ABX is far more than just marketing. **ABX and Total Customer Growth are part of a business philosophy that covers the whole customer journey.**

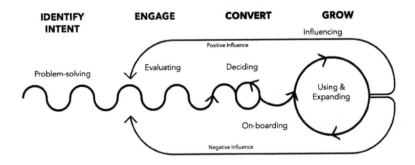

In our view, ABX includes the practices involved in using ABM techniques to acquire customers, but it goes beyond that. ABX includes how you grow and retain those customers once you have acquired them and how you turn them into evangelists for your business. It also includes identifying at-risk customers and getting them back on track.

ABX-Driven Culture Change

To begin, let's look into how ABX affects the culture of how a company sells and markets.

We have observed that as companies adopt ABM as a better way to market, moving up to ABX becomes a natural progression. As an organization adopts it more deeply, something more fundamental happens.

We recently sat down with the CMO of a leading health care technology firm—a telehealth tech company that targets and markets to health care providers. This company undertook an ABM program in 2021 that included implementing Demandbase.

It was challenging to shift toward an ABM model, but it took hold in the second year. Most notably, thanks to the CMOs' conviction, the CEO became a big proponent and supporter of the culture shift in how they marketed.

The CMO spoke about the impact ABM was having across target accounts and the current customer base. The CEO could see how it was changing the way they approached cross-selling and upselling. It was transforming how they thought about the whole customer life cycle.

This is ABX in action.

The Trifecta: Marketing, Sales, and Customer Success

The single most important factor in ABM's success or failure is the alignment between marketing and sales. Alignment among marketing, sales, and customer success is critical to ABX's success.

Marketing owns generating demand, sales is responsible for converting demand (opportunity) to revenue, and customer success owns the relationship with the customer. This is especially important in ABX, as customer satisfaction is a significant factor in the customer's buying additional products and services and being your advocate to future customers.

In the next chapter, we dive into why it is important to have insight into existing accounts. Many organizations deploy customer sentiment tools, like Gainsight, to track and measure customer success to understand the state of the current customer base. They have red, yellow, and green flags for customers and use Net Promoter Score (NPS). Customer success uses this knowledge to increase customer retention and reduce churn. When implemented well, these tools can give you insights that support an ABX model. This includes whether customers are likely to defect or are happy but looking for additional products or services they are unaware you provide.

Regarding ABX, the challenge is that sales, marketing, and customer success tend to operate in silos.

Collaboration is infrequent and requires a culture change. Your CEO, therefore, is critical in instilling the importance of this collaboration in making ABX a reality. Typically, the CMO is the change agent, though. In many cases, this disconnect requires new skills and a new approach to building the bridge across the departments.

How This Changes the Role of Marketing

Being an ABM-savvy B2B marketer requires four fundamental superpowers:

- Customer insights
- Brand-building
- Demand generation
- Tech savviness

First and foremost, you need to be an expert on your customers. You need to understand how they buy, what's important to them, and what critical insight can help you sell to them more effectively.

The second superpower is being a brand strategist. You are the custodian of the brand and its positioning, identity, and image. You sweat about brand awareness, including social media, website, logo design, fonts, colors, social media activity, and, of course, advertising.

The third, being a demand generator, means you are focused on generating leads. You look at pipeline and leads, then you figure out how to drive more.

The fourth is being a savvy technologist. You look at technology to help run marketing more efficiently and more effectively, and you use data to make decisions about your direction. You may become an expert in marketing automation and the various platforms that can help with that.

There is now a new skill you must master: ABX. In many regards, ABX is a fusion of all these skills. As you are trying to generate additional demand among new and existing customers, you have to be an expert in the customer life cycle. Consider how your existing customers affect your brand and master new technologies and data to be successful.

Customer Life-Cycle Thinking

As we cover in Chapter 2, marketing's primary role in ABM is attracting qualified opportunities. In ABX, marketing employees need to think about the whole customer life cycle, becoming experts in how marketing can help customer success address satisfaction issues and help sales upsell and cross-sell.

Early in the customer life cycle, marketing's priority is building brand awareness, making sure prospects see the value you can deliver and how you can solve their problems. You are then focused on helping sales convert interested in-market prospects that are showing intent and seem to have an active buying cycle going on. Once they convert and become a customer, you work with customer success to ensure they stay happy and continue to see your value based on what they are experiencing. You work with sales to identify other departments that could use the products or services you sell. And finally, you determine whether customers will advocate for you to prospects or harm your reputation. If any seem likely to do harm, you must develop strategies to address it.

Full customer life cycle thinking becomes especially important during a recession. When times are tough, marketing budgets are typically the first to be cut. This is primarily in anticipation of low demand, especially from new customers.

In difficult economic times, ABX is more important than ever for shifting the focus to retaining and growing current customers. After all, it is four to ten times easier to get additional business from existing customers than it is to acquire new ones.

In the past, many marketers have seen customer success and current customers as an afterthought. We now see marketers putting more energy into protecting their current customers and finding ways to upsell or cross-sell to them. And marketing, sales, and customer success are starting to come together more closely during tighter financial times.

Taking the Lead toward Better Collaboration

So, how do you get everybody working on the same page, especially when they are all working off different playbooks?

In ABX, everyone must have the same playbook. They must be looking at the same data and the same reports. Ideally, you should have a single dashboard that shows the team what's happening with current customers, in certain industries and segments, and with potential prospects.

One dashboard is critical in getting everyone working toward the same outcome. Alignment across the different departments really matters. Historically, marketing, sales, and customer success have been very siloed. Now, they all need to come together with a formal alignment and operating process.

In many cases, marketing will need to take the lead in building alignment cross-functionally across these three groups. They should gain alignment from sales, SDRs, and customer success on their activities.

There should be a standing cadence running among these groups. Every company does this differently, but these groups should talk about that alignment at least monthly, discussing their campaigns, what they are seeing in intent and across their current customers, and what is going on with new prospects.

You will want to maintain a routine of reviewing KPIs and continue having general discussions about how you are progressing with ABX in general.

A standard cadence of meeting at least monthly to gain that alignment can validate what is going on as you think about current campaigns and how to make sure you are all working off the same playbook and toward the same goal.

This will translate into planning routines. Typically, you will create a quarterly plan (at least) for ABX. Why? Because things change so rapidly. You need to be able to adjust and pivot based on what you are seeing and the changes in trends. That way, if you see a big spike in intent for a particular industry, such as financial services, you can pivot to address industry-specific, product-specific, or problem-specific issues.

You might also look at lost opportunities as a team. Discuss whether you can bring any of those customers back if buyer's remorse sets in. You may be surprised at how you can source net new opportunities when a prospect goes with the competitor, only to come back because they are unhappy with the implementation.

Keys to Success

As you envision ABX in your organization, several things will be key to your success:

- A holistic view of the customer life cycle and a belief that working across the entire customer life cycle leads to more profitable customers

- Executive buy-in on a commitment to move toward ABX (Ideally, the CEO provides support and a vision for this.)
- Alignment among marketing, sales, and customer success (All three need to work toward a common goal using the same playbook, agreed-upon, common KPIs, and the same system to measure progress.)
- Accurate and actionable insight about your accounts, including an understanding of who your advocate is and who may be a defector

• • •

We go into this last issue in depth next. It is a big deal. In most companies, account insight is siloed in the sales team or even known by individual salespeople. To be successful in Total Customer Growth, you have to get a good handle on customer insight. The next chapter covers what good customer insight looks like and how you get it.

> Go to https://learn.totalcustomergrowth.com to access resources for this chapter including the Total Customer Growth Planning Framework. You can use it as you read this book.

CHAPTER 12

Account Insight-Driven Growth

What You Will Learn in This Chapter

- What account insight is and what the different types are
- Why the Net Promoter Score (NPS) has its limitations in B2B markets
- Ten steps to gather better account insight
- How to use intent data to strengthen account insight
- Multiple ways to turn account insights into action toward Total Customer Growth

The Total Customer Growth Framework is as much about growing existing customers as it is about using ABM techniques to win new ones. In this chapter, we focus on the foundation of any existing customer growth strategy: account insight

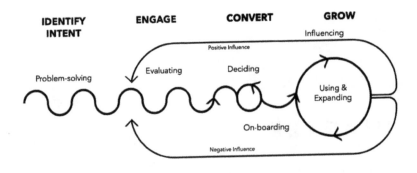

Different Types of Account Insight

> "... as we know, there are known knowns; there are things we know we know. We also know there are known unknowns; that is to say, we know there are some things we do not know. But there are also unknown unknowns—the ones we don't know, we don't know ..." Donald Rumsfeld

As we all know, it is much easier—typically four to ten times easier—to win more business from a current customer than to win and get business from new customers. And the more you know about your customers, the better you will do at growing revenues with them.

Let's dive into account insight: what it is and how to be more knowledgeable about how committed your customers are, what their future needs are, how likely they are to give you business, and how to be more successful with them.

There are many different ways to get better intelligence about what is happening with existing customers.

The best-known methodology is the Net Promoter Score (NPS), which is based on a single question: How likely is the customer to recommend your company?

It is a simple way to survey for satisfaction across your clients. But in our view, it has severe limitations in B2B.

Limitations of Net Promoter Score (NPS)

NPS has made a significant impact in helping companies improve customer satisfaction. It is especially effective in B2C businesses, where you are marketing and selling to individuals who are often the direct product users.

The premise of NPS is that a single question—How likely are you to recommend this product to a friend?—is a proxy for satisfaction, especially when the respondents give feedback on why they gave the answer they did.

NPS works well in B2C markets, but it is hard to make it work as effectively in B2B.

If you get user feedback on your product, NPS may be fine. However, if you are trying to get a clear picture of all customer satisfaction, NPS has shortcomings.

Why? There are many different stakeholders involved. This means you need to get a representative sample from the key stakeholders and gather sufficient feedback so your team can develop a plan to act on the feedback.

The common problem with NPS we hear about is that survey participation can be low, and feedback is shallow and hard to act on. In addition, when the sample does not represent all key stakeholders, the responses are biased and may be misleading.

You may need feedback from the C-suite, VPs, directors, and managers to get a complete picture of how well you are positioned in your accounts. If your responses are primarily from managers and very few of the VPs in the C-suite respond, your picture of the state of your relationships is skewed toward the managers' opinions. You may get a rosy picture from the managers without knowing that senior executives, who manage budgets and decide on solutions, are starting to look elsewhere.

NPS is a good leading indicator of customer satisfaction, but you need to go deeper.

In the words of Carey Evans, from Relationship Audits™, a firm that specializes in customer commitment measurement. Measuring commitment goes beyond measuring satisfaction, "It can tell you that a bomb is about to go off in the neighborhood but not precisely where it is and how to defuse it."

The other issue is that satisfied clients are not necessarily committed clients. In his book *The Loyalty Effect: The Hidden Force Behind Growth, Profits, and Lasting Value*, Frederick Reichheld, the creator of NPS, says that 60% to 80% of customers who said they were satisfied defected to another vendor. So, if your customer satisfaction survey tells you that your clients are satisfied, do not get comfortable. The odds are that they are open to a competitor's offer.

10 Steps to Gather Insights about Your Customers and Turn Them into Growth

Ideally, in assessing customer satisfaction, you will determine several critical things:

- Which customers are committed
- Which customers are at risk of defection
- What you need to do to serve them better
- How to grow your business with your customers

It is hard to imagine more important information than this!

So, how do you do this effectively?

The following is what we regard as best practice. It looks like a great deal of work, and that is because it is. However, it is much less work than dealing with the consequences of a surprise defection.

If you do this well, it can transform your business. But poorly executed customer insights and satisfaction assessments can, at best, tell you very little. They may even relay false information that can mislead your strategy.

Here are the recommended ten steps:

1. **Create a formal client assessment project** - Resolve to make this issue a high priority. Formalize the process by having your firm's leadership team endorse it (or better yet, initiate it). Get buy-in from all the key executives on your side so that they support this.

2. **Prioritize candidate customers for assessments** - Get feedback from the customers who represent at least 50% of your revenues in aggregate. Talk with any customer whose departure would create significant turmoil. Prioritize customers that represent the greatest potential growth and those that would create the greatest damage if they left.

3. **Determine your best method for the assessment** - If you need to get feedback from only 10 to 20 or so clients across your top customers, you could get detailed feedback through in-person or phone interviews. If you need more clients than that, interviews may be impractical. In this case, you could use an online survey, easily done yourself through a tool like SurveyMonkey. Relationship Audits has a very robust way of

doing it. You may want to consider a mix of both—online for the mid- to junior-level participants, and phone-based for the most important and senior stakeholders.

4. **Get your clients' buy-in** - Most clients will appreciate that you are doing this to make sure you are addressing their needs, especially if you position it as a proactive initiative to ensure that you have the right resources in place. But if they do not want to participate, it could be a warning sign. Be concerned.

5. **Design a survey that will uncover the truth about your relationships** - You are unlikely to get sufficient information with two or three questions. In our experience, you will not uncover the truth with fewer than ten questions, especially in an online survey. The question set should include their likelihood to recommend you, their priorities for next year, how well you delivered against expectations, what they think you do best, what they think you should improve on, and what changes they would like to see.

6. **Aim for more than 75% participation** - If you are conducting this as an online assessment, it is very hard to get 100% participation. It is not impossible, but it is a steep hill to climb. In our experience, 75% is high enough to get reliable insights about the state of your key relationships. The key is to achieve a representative sample across your customer stakeholders. This means you need to employ a survey system that can send out multiple reminders and track who has not responded, so you can reach them in a more targeted way, which might include asking their boss to nudge them to respond or making a personal outreach.

7. **Review findings internally and be objective** - Have a process to discuss the findings with your leadership team. Avoid blame in adverse situations. Be positive and constructive in how you will make improvements. Best of all, where you have

identified positive findings, figure out how you can use these insights to gain more business

8. **Present your findings to the client** - Once the process is complete, it is critical to review with your clients what you have learned and, most importantly, share with them an action plan for what you are going to do about it.

9. **Check back later on progress** - After six months, check back with the senior clients to determine how you are progressing with the action plan.

10. **Rinse and repeat** - Plan on performing this process annually. It conveys to the client that you are committed to a long-term relationship that is underpinned by continuous improvement.

Again, this may seem like hard work, but take it from us: it works. Here is Adam's personal story:

In the mid-2000s, I was a senior executive at a marketing services firm. I was responsible for one of the firm's largest accounts.

When we first won the business, the fees were relatively small, but this account had great potential. We decided to invest in the account and hired an outside consultant to help assess how we were positioned and how to grow the business.

This consultant conducted in-depth, one-on-one interviews with a dozen executives at the client organization.

The findings were positive. They were satisfied with our service and identified some improvements. Most importantly, they provided us with a clear path to what we could do to help them over the next few years. This translated into a significant growth path for us.

We used this insight to develop a growth strategy. It included changing up some of the staff on the account and raising the level of thought leadership we provided. This paid off.

Through a long-term strategy, we increased our revenues with this client ten times over five years. This tactic included having the outside consultant interview the stakeholders every year.

In years three, four, and five, this method identified some warning signs. I left the business in year five, and, sadly, the firm lost the account sometime later. Many factors went into this loss, but not adequately addressing the warning signs was a significant contributing factor.

Using Intent Data with Customers

Before we examine how to turn insights into action, let's review how intent data can provide additional insight.

As we cover in Chapter 3, intent data is like magic! It can tell you what a prospect is interested in months before they engage with you. It can help you create an effective ABM program to influence them way before they ever meet with you.

It is also critical in ABX and can help you with your existing customers. Here are two use cases.

- **Identifying upsell opportunities** - We recently used intent data with a client and saw positive results within a week. Their SDR team was researching current customer intent for a relatively new service the client was offering. The head of the SDR team saw that a very large current customer was showing intent for this service but had not purchased it from them. She alerted the account team, and within a few days, they reached the right person at the customer, who said they were about to start an RFP process and would include the client.

- **Identifying at-risk customers** - While the most exciting use of intent data is finding new customers, it is also valuable in keeping an eye on existing ones. For example, if you are in a wireless networking company, you can create a report that tracks what your current customers are interested in. If you see they are actively surging for wireless networking or one of your competitors as topics, it indicates they are looking around.

How to Turn Insights into Action

The ABX Trifecta

The number-one factor in converting insights about our customers into a growth strategy is a seamless collaboration among customer success, sales, and marketing.

Your customer success team is responsible for the care and feeding of your customers. Their primary measure of performance should be how well they address customer satisfaction issues. Many factors go into this, but in terms of ABX and customer growth, their relationship with sales and marketing is critical.

Sales will be responsible for revenue expansion from existing customers. In some organizations, account managers are sales representatives who focus exclusively on existing customers. Customer success is part of their role.

Regardless, someone needs to focus on what it takes to make a customer committed, and someone needs to be responsible for growing revenue per customer. Marketing should support the needs of both.

In some organizations, marketing runs a customer satisfaction survey. It is their responsibility primarily because marketing tends to be more experienced in customer research. Marketing may also analyze intent data. In addition, they should partner with customer success and sales to develop ways to grow revenue with existing customers. For example, what thought leadership content should be developed to address issues raised by existing customers? Should there be events exclusively for existing customers? Which customers will provide testimonials or be references?

Segment Your Customers

The first step in developing a growth strategy with your existing customers is to reevaluate how you segment them. For example, use your satisfaction survey to put them in one of four buckets:

- **Committed** - Customers that account for significant revenue, say they are happy with you, and indicate a long-term commitment
- **At risk** - Customers that account for significant revenue, have indicated they are dissatisfied, and may be at risk of defection
- **Growth candidates** - Customers that account for lower revenue but could spend more with you and have indicated they are happy with you
- **Maintenance** - Customers that account for lower revenue and are neutral or dissatisfied with you

Strategies

- **Convert committed into evangelists** - In short, your committed customer relationships are extraordinarily valuable in helping you acquire new customers. In the next chapter, we cover how to do this. For now, though, here are some strategies for at-risk clients:
  - Take short-term actions to address flight risks. Your most urgent priority is fixing relationships with at-risk, high-value customers.
  - Communicate that you have heard them and are acting on their feedback. It helps if this comes from a senior executive, possibly even your CEO.
  - Develop a specific and detailed action plan about how you will address the negative issues. This should include what you need from them to be successful.
  - Schedule check-ins to discuss how you are progressing.
  - Suggest running an assessment with these customers at the six-month mark to get formal feedback on how you have addressed the issues.
  - If you are using third-party intent data, track these accounts for intent data topics related to what you provide. If you see spikes around what you do for them, this could be a warning sign that they are actively looking to switch.
- **Determine upsell opportunities** - If you designed your customer satisfaction assessment effectively, you will have insights from these customers on what they need and what problems they need help with.
  - This is the basis of a plan to grow your revenues with these customers. It may not give you all the answers, but it creates an opening.

- o Your customer success and account managers should return to these customers and thank them for participating, review what you have learned, and ask them to clarify. Doing this will get them to expand on their needs, creating possible upsell opportunities. Use it to ensure that they know about all the other things you can provide them with.
- o Ask for introductions to other departments that may be interested in solutions you can provide.
- o Tell them about your product road map. This input can help you pre-sell them upcoming solutions.

- **Work with marketing** - Use these insights to create new content and marketing campaigns that address these opportunities.
- **Monitor maintenance clients** - These are the customers you would prefer not to lose but expect to either grow or churn. The key is to keep monitoring them and determine which ones can move up to growth candidates at some point.

Regarding your ABX program, the last thing is to revisit your buyer journeys. Incorporate what you have learned into their questions and needs, content that would appeal to them, and how to engage them.

● ● ●

In our next chapter, we provide ideas and strategies for improving the influence your current customers have on new-customer acquisition.

Go to https://learn.totalcustomergrowth.com to access resources for this chapter including a guide on how to design customer interview process that will uncover account insights.

CHAPTER 13

Turning Customers into Positive Influencers

What You Will Learn in This Chapter

- Why your customers are a critical part of your marketing strategy
- How to develop a listening program
- How to create a Total Customer Growth program using influencer marketing with your existing customers

When most people think about influencer marketing, the first example that comes to mind is B2C, but it is at least equally effective in B2B. It should also be a key consideration in your Total Customer Growth strategy.

As we describe in Chapter 2, your customers are important influencers—positive or negative—in your pipeline of prospective new customers.

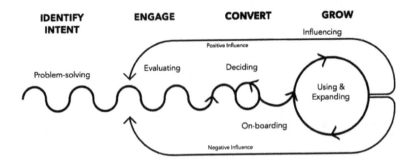

Your current customers are significant in influencer marketing because **people trust other people more than they do any other channel**. According to Nielsen's Global Trust in Advertising report (2021), 89% of people globally trust recommendations from friends and family.

Interestingly, branded websites are the second-most-trusted channel. This fact reinforces why sharing customer testimonials on your website and other forms of social proof should be a high priority.

In developing a buyer-journey-driven marketing strategy, you should assume that buyers will talk to peers and actively seek their opinions as they consider solutions. They will also rely on sources of reviews and ratings, which may include analysts, rating websites, social media, or any public source of customer reviews.

Ignore this at your peril!

Companies that have mastered influencer marketing use it to build trust and turn trust into committed relationships.

Listening

The foundation of influencer marketing with your customers is understanding what they are saying about you or not saying about you. There are several ways to assess this.

Social Media Listening Programs

Many services empower you to monitor what people are saying about you online. Services like Sprout Social and Meltwater enable you to analyze sentiments about your brand. You can determine what positive things are being said, what the negative topics are, and what is being said about you versus your competitors.

It is important to determine who the strongest influencers are, especially if they are customers. Most importantly, try to analyze comments by customers.

Comparison Sites

One of the more structured forms of social influence are comparison and rating sites. Sites like G2, Capterra, and Software Advice make it easy for buyers to compare solutions based on customer ratings.

It is easy to have your company rated, and these channels are also good channels for digital marketing.

Analysts

B2B firms have love/hate relationships with market analysts. Some companies feel you have to pay for an expensive subscription to be covered by an analyst. However, B2B buyers hold analyst firms like Gartner and Forrester in high regard.

Again, ignore them at your peril.

In the context of ABX, the most important analysts base their perspectives entirely on customer interviews. For example, in health care technology, the analyst firm KLAS Research surveys vendors' customers to create market analyses on different sectors within health care. Buyers value their reports, when analyzing how their peers are addressing similar issues and how they rate various vendors.

As a vendor, this knowledge is important in gauging how you compare to your competitors and understanding what your customers and prospects value as important. It can also help provide ideas and prioritization advice on what to consider in your product road map.

Intent Data

As we cover in prior chapters, use intent data with your current customers to understand what other solutions they are evaluating and determine who is at risk of defecting.

Influencer Marketing Strategies

So, how do you use intelligence about your customers to influence your prospects? Here are several strategies to consider:

The Basics

There are several elements you should consider as "basic hygiene" in marketing:

- **Logos as social proof** - As you have no doubt noticed, most B2B websites feature their customers' logos prominently. These are important, as when a buyer visits a website, one of their first questions will be, "Do they have customers like me?"
- **Testimonials** - These extend basic social proof into showing how committed your customers are and providing clear examples of what it is like to work with you.

- **Case studies** - These are especially helpful to buyers later in the buyer journey. They are important for your champion prospects, as they provide substantial detail on what to expect. Champions use these case studies with their buyer committees. Case studies are also great PR ammunition. Trade publications love to write detailed stories about how a company in the market they cover has solved a problem. Your case studies make that easier for them.

- **References** - Later in the buying process, prospects will ask to speak to references they can interview privately about why they should select you. It is best to have a large pool of these who are ready to go. You do not want to depend on a few customers who may begrudge you asking them too often.

Create Customer Champions

Customers will become even more enthusiastic about you when you celebrate them. There are so many ways to do that. These will all require that sales and marketing partner with the customer success team.

- Identify your most committed customers and design a customer champion program around them. This will include several different strategies. Celebrate their wins by reposting and tagging when your customers are featured in the press or social media. This awareness shows you care about them and their success. It also associates you with their success.

- Make them proud to be your customer by giving them advance notice when good news is about to break. For example, let them know when you are winning an award, making a major hire, or closing a funding round. Giving them these alerts increases the likelihood that they will share this in social media.

- Share a case study and tag the company and individual customers when you write a post on LinkedIn or Twitter about customer accomplishments. This will expose your post to their network and extend the reach of your social media post.

- Celebrate them. This will make your most committed and enthusiastic supporters more open to advocating for you. They, too, have egos and are ambitious about their careers, so many will be open to being featured in the media on your behalf. Create a campaign around them that features them speaking about you in press stories, webinars, social media posts, testimonial videos, and on conference panels that you host.

- If you can afford it, host an annual customer event where you invite customers, prospects, and partners. Celebrate your customers and tell their stories to demonstrate your solutions' impacts. Introduce them in person to prospects. They cannot help but evangelize what you do in a setting like this.

- Encourage and make it easy for them to post about these events on social media. This is also important in converting neutral and negatively disposed customers. For customers that seem satisfied but not committed, these events are an opportunity to showcase the value of what you do and expose them to benefits they may not know about. For at-risk customers, it may be an opportunity for special attention and a forum for senior executives to hear their concerns.

Educate Your Customers

So much of the content created in B2B marketing is geared toward new-customer acquisition. But your existing customers are also a critical audience. Seeing you as an authority will make them value you more. Thought-leadership content that reinforces your knowledge and insight will educate them and reinforce that they made a good decision.

It also gives them content to share on social media and pass along to their peers. You can make this strategy more effective by having them contribute to this content.

Invite Them into Your Product Development Process

One of the best things you can do to turn customers into evangelists is to formally include them in your product development process. Customer and user advisory boards are good mechanisms for this. These let your product development leaders to hear directly from customers about what they would like included.

> **Important:** As you deploy new features, publicly acknowledge your customers' input and give them advance notice of updates. Remind them that they contributed to this development. Tag them with thanks in social media posts announcing launches. This will increase the reach and likelihood of customers sharing your posts.

Neutralize Negative News

Bad news travels faster than good news. So, when a customer complains about you online, you have to jump on it ASAP! This is one of the reasons it is so important to have a social listening team in place. The key is to have a procedure to address negativity.

You cannot do anything to reverse a legitimate negative post, but you may be able to stop additional ones. Marketing and customer success will need to work closely together.

First, customer success needs to acknowledge to the customer that you take their concern(s) seriously and offer to address the issue as fast as possible. Organize a team to meet with them quickly. Make sure that team includes a senior executive and other executives who can help resolve this issue. Then, put a remediation plan in place.

This will both put you on track to solve the issue and likely dissuade the customer from posting negative comments about you while you resolve the issue.

• • •

Influencer marketing and relationship-building strategies are key parts of your long-term growth strategies. In an ABX program, they are some of the most powerful tools in your arsenal to influence future sales with new customers.

In Part 4, we help you develop a long-term road map to Total Customer Growth, so you can get moving and get scaling.

Go to https://learn.totalcustomergrowth.com to access resources for this chapter including a webinar on how to create an influencer marketing program.

PART 4

Get Moving.
Get Scaling.

What You Will Learn in Part 4

In the previous chapters, we laid the foundation and showed you how to build a plan, evolve to Total Customer Growth, implement ABM campaigns, and move from ABM to a more holistic ABX model. In the final part of this book, we show you how to build an organization driven by the Total Customer Growth Model.

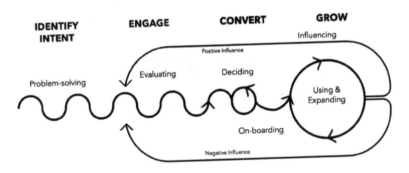

We start with how to get moving. Overcoming inertia is surprisingly difficult.

OK, change is hard, but the transition to ABM seems intuitive. It feels more like an evolution than a revolution. However, many organizations struggle to get started down the ABM journey. And when they do get started, their efforts are often quite tentative, especially in the first year or so.

Here is how Part 4 is structured:

- In Chapter 14 we introduce you to Think/Crawl/Walk/Run and get you started with your first pilot.
- Chapter 15 is all about scaling and evolving. We provide you with a strategic framework to achieve that.
- Chapter 16 is a slight detour into Agile marketing—an important concept and skill that will help you scale your Total Customer Growth approach.
- Lastly, in Chapter 17, we paint a vision for what Total Customer Growth looks like in action and what the key skills are for leading the change toward this vision.

CHAPTER 14

Think/Crawl/Walk/Run

What You Will Learn in This Chapter

- About Think/Crawl/Walk/Run
- How to create a high-level road map for your first 12 to 18 months
- How to design and run a pilot
- How to create your ABM playbook

This chapter should equip you with the tools and initial steps to get moving.

But first, an important question:

Is it worth taking the first step?

The short answer: Yes!

ABM works.

According to the ITSMA ABM Benchmark report in 2021, across 300 ABM practitioners, 72% of companies that use ABM report it delivers a higher ROI than other strategies. Seventy percent said it was influencing all their marketing. And 50% said it was helping the company become more customer centric. In addition, 61% reported that ABM was leading to better sales and marketing alignment.

While ABM accounted for 27% of marketing budgets, 75% of companies planned to increase their ABM budget in 2022. Companies also saw a shift in budget spend in 2022 from traditional marketing—like virtual trade shows, public relations (PR), and search engine marketing—to their ABM budget, due to the direct ROI and revenue when executed properly.

The good news: If you get started now, you will not be early to the ABM party, but you are not late either. Instead, you may be just in time if you are in B2B.

We talk to dozens of B2B firms every year, and most have not yet adopted ABM. To put it in context, fewer than 5,000 companies use one of the top four ABM platforms. By comparison, HubSpot has well over 100,000 customers. So, while ABM is seen as the future of B2B marketing, relatively few companies have taken the big step and fully embraced an ABM strategy.

Even among those that do practice ABM, most are not far along in their usage. According to the ITSMA study, more than half of the ABM practitioners reported they were still either experimenting, piloting, or just exploring ABM. Only 13% reported that ABM is embedded in what they do and how they market and sell.

When we speak with firms that report using ABM, we find they frequently use a few ABM tactics or principles but have not rolled out the strategy as part of the foundation for their marketing and selling efforts.

The point is that if you have not started down the ABM path or are early in your journey, you are not alone.

But becoming experts in ABM can give you a significant competitive advantage.

Think/Crawl/Walk/Run

If you have done any research on ABM, you will have heard of Crawl/Walk/Run. The rationale is that ABM is hard and takes a long time to perfect. The journey requires the buy-in and active participation of many colleagues. And you will need to constantly remind everyone about what you are undertaking on this journey.

It is easy to procrastinate. There is always something more urgent that requires attention. And when you do get started with ABM, there will be challenges, disappointments, and distractions, all of which will make you want to pause or cancel the program and go back to more traditional marketing.

The notion of Crawl/Walk/Run provides a framework that helps you break down the journey into major steps. Crawl is about exploring and experimenting. Walk occurs when you have validated the value of ABM and started to make ABM an integral part of how you market. Run is when ABM and ABX become embedded in your organization. It is *how* you sell and market.

We added a preparation stage to this, which we call "Think." Why?

You will struggle or fail if you start crawling without thinking through what you are trying to achieve in the pilot, the prerequisites that are needed, what the longer-term road map looks like, what it will take to be successful, and important strategic issues to avoid.

You most likely realize this. As a strategic marketer, you know it is a risk, and this is the root cause of why you may have hesitated to get going or are struggling with ABM.

To that end, in Think you will develop a high-level road map that creates a vision for how you may adopt ABM as an organization. You will design a pilot as a first step. In designing this pilot, you will create an ABM playbook that will guide the pilot.

Think

Define your ABM/ABX strategy in less than six weeks with the Account-based Marketing Playbook

Crawl

Generate demand and learn how to get an Account-based Marketing working with a 90-day Pilot

Walk

Scale ABM across the organization and see your entire team increase demand and productivity

Run

Transition from ABM to ABX and make your highest value customers even more profitable

We cover the Think and Crawl stages in this chapter and Walk and Run in separate chapters.

Think

There are two big issues to resolve in the Think stage: your long-term Total Customer Growth vision to become an ABM- and ABX-driven organization and what you will do in the near term to start the journey. The first part is about creating a high-level road map that explains how your organization can make a Total Customer Growth Model (i.e., *the specific* ways you will market, sell, and support customers). The short-term vision is about designing a time-bound pilot that allows you to experiment with ABM.

You can download examples and templates at learn.totalcustomergrowth.com.

Long-Term Road-Mapping

There are many ways to lay out a long-term vision. Think/Crawl/Walk/Run provides a simple framework. We suggest you create a short document for your executive team that includes:

- A definition of Total Customer Growth, ABM, and ABX.
- Examples of how ABM and ABX could improve marketing, sales, and customer success performance. The findings from the ITSMA Benchmark Study will show how companies are seeing improved marketing ROI.
- The Total Customer Growth Model to visually explain the long-term vision of how you will transform the customer journey.
- The journey you are proposing:
    - **Think** - How you are developing a strategy to initiate the ABM journey.
    - **Crawl** - How you will experiment with ABM in a time-bound way, with examples of two or three pilots you are considering.
    - **Walk** - How you will start to implement ABM and ABX across the organization, possibly including a timeline of how they could be deployed by business unit.
    - **Run** - A narrative that tells the story of how your organization could grow in a more efficient and higher-performing way using the Total Customer Growth Model. Consider using vignettes of how different parts of the business will sell and market differently.
- A clear explanation of the risks and challenges. Above all, explain that this is a long-term initiative that will take patience and persistence to perfect. Your executive team must

understand this is a transformational change, not just a new marketing fad.

- A request for support from the executive team, and especially the CEO. You will need this air cover as you start the journey.

Additionally, how you measure marketing may need to change if you are still focused on metrics like MQLs and leads as measures of marketing's success. ABM and ABX will have a direct impact on overall revenue as a result of a successful ABM program. Marketing teams should move to being measured on overall company revenue, customer growth, and customer retention as their goals and be 100% aligned to the sales and customer success objectives in the business. This step will also help with alignment and prioritization across these groups.

Pilot Selection

Your next task is to determine a pilot to experiment with this new model. The right pilot is a time-bound way to test how ABM principles will change sales and marketing in your organization.

You need to be realistic in selecting a pilot that you can run in a short period, typically 90 days, and for which you can measure results. However, you should also have enough ambition to select a pilot that can show how ABM will make a bigger impact. If your goal is too small, your colleagues may not be convinced about ABM's potential regardless of outcome.

One way to select a pilot is to break your sales cycle into 90-day phases. For example, if your typical sales cycle lasts nine months, break it into three 90-day phases. The initial 90 days is typically when sales and marketing focus on generating new qualified opportunities. In the second 90 days, you will focus on moving the deal through the pipeline. In the last 90 days, sales will primarily focus on deal size and rate of conversion to a closed deal.

These three phases present three possible pilot opportunities:

- **Opportunity generation (pipeline)** - How can you use ABM to create better-qualified opportunities more efficiently?
- **Deal velocity** - How can ABM help increase sales velocity and shorten the time from opportunity to revenue?
- **Conversion** - Can ABM improve the deal size and conversion rate?

It may be apparent here that the first is easier to implement and measure in 90 days. An ABM pilot typically focuses on demand generation of new customer opportunities. The nice thing is that it will start the conversation about how ABM works throughout the entire sales process.

Before moving on to pilot design, it's important to note that ABM principles are as important in growing existing customers as winning new logos is. You may also consider a pilot by finding products or services existing customers are not currently using and cross-selling or upselling into them.

Pilot Design

Once you have selected your pilot, it is time to plan what you will do in 90 days. We suggest you break this into four sequential tasks:

1. **Goal-setting** - Measurable goals you can achieve in 90 days. (Example: Net new pipeline sourced using intent data.)
2. **Target definition** - Accounts you will target and data you will need to target them. (Examples: Intent topics and pain points.)

3. **Pilot definition** - The components of the pilot, tactics you will use, content you need, and anything new you need to execute this. (Examples: A customer case study, video, or infographic.)

4. **90-day plan** - A detailed project plan, including the most important component of all—the person from your organization who will be involved in the pilot and contribute to developing and executing it. (Examples: Marketing operations lead, marketing ABM owner, sales lead, and customer success lead.)

Let's dive into each of these in more detail.

Goal Setting

We like the SMART framework in setting goals, especially for a pilot. If you are not familiar with this, SMART goals are:

- **S**pecific
- **M**easurable
- **A**ttainable
- **R**ealistic (we often combine Attainable and Realistic)
- **T**ime-bound

Here is an example of a SMART goal framework:

Specific	To close 5 deals this year, we need to grow the pipeline of opportunities by 25% by end of Q2
Measurable	• 25 qualified opportunities • $1M in ABM-sourced pipeline • TAL engagement 100%
Attainable and Realistic	This goal is achievable if we focus our marketing on in-market prospects only
Time-bound	90 days

As you can see, the goal is specific and is in the context of a bigger sales goal. It is measurable in terms of qualified opportunities, pipeline dollar amount, and TAL engagement. The latter is the most interesting, as it is a way to determine if engagement from your TAL is any different than engagement from other campaigns. You will focus the campaign on in-market prospects, which makes it an ABM campaign, and you are time-bounding this to a 90-day project.

Target Definition

Here, you select which target accounts you will create an ABM campaign for. By definition, this will determine whether you will do a 1:1, 1:Few, or 1:Many campaign. As you will see in the examples below, you can pilot any of the three types.

It is key to test for your ability to identify in-market and best-fit customers. If you are using third-party intent data, it is possible to run a 1:Many campaign, where you target a large number of in-market accounts. If you do not have access to third-party intent data, we suggest you restrict yourself to a smaller set of accounts and run a 1:1 campaign to fewer than 20 accounts or a 1:Few campaign to fewer than 100 accounts.

The second factor in determining who you will target is the ability to define a best-fit account. You may want to make determining how to identify best-fit accounts part of your pilot. For example, as secondary goals in your pilot, consider trying to answer these questions:

- What do you wish you knew that would help you determine best-fit accounts?
- What would help you narrow down your best-fit accounts? For example, which accounts are showing the strongest buying

signals, which accounts would make a great customer, are they financially strong, do they have a greater need, what is your ability to sell to them, and have you successfully sold to other similar accounts before?

- What data would help you determine who is in-market? This answer could include your own deal and sales history, firmographics, buyer behavior on your website, social media, and, of course, third-party intent data.

Use this analysis to decide who you will target. Try to be as precise as possible. In the examples below, a firm piloted ABM by targeting accounts that had switched ERP systems and consequently would have a greater unmet need for services. They created a list of about 100 accounts that had switched ERP systems in the past year.

Pilot Definition

We suggest that you create a document for this. The pilot definition document will include the following:

- **Team** - Who will be part of the team? The pilot MUST include sales and marketing team members. One of your stealth goals is to determine alignment issues. We strongly suggest you get your SDRs involved, as we explain in Chapter 9.
- **Flavor of ABM** - Will you be piloting a 1:1, 1: Few, or 1:Many ABM? This will largely be determined by your target definition.
- **Target accounts** - What is the list of target accounts? What are their characteristics?
- **Buyer journeys** - If you have not already created buyer personas and buyer journeys, this is a good opportunity to do that.

- **Engagement strategy** - How will you engage the personas? What tactics will you use? This may be an opportunity to try out some new tactics. Refer to Chapter 7 for inspiration here.
- **Required and available assets** - What content will you need? What content do you have available? Do you need to create additional content for the pilot? What data do you have and need? See ideas in Chapter 6.
- **Required and available technology** - How can you implement the pilot without any new technology? This is not the time to implement an ABM platform. This is when you want to test out ABM principles with what you already have.
- **Measurement plan** - How will you know if you are successful? What KPIs will you use to measure how the pilot performed? Most importantly, what measures will provide insight into how to improve performance? Refer to Chapter 10 for ideas.
- **Budget** - Last but not least, how much will this cost? Ideally, you can execute within your overall annual plan and budget.

Congratulations! You have just created your first ABM playbook. We discuss the ABM playbook in more detail in the next chapter.

Crawl

Now, you are ready to go. But remember these things:

- Keep it simple.
- Leverage what assets you already have.
- Do not forget: You are looking to evaluate whether ABM is a good strategy to pursue, NOT deliver a massive ROI. (At least not yet.)
- This is step 1 on the journey.

As you move into implementation, we suggest you develop a simple project plan. Break up the activities over the 90 days into 30-day bursts. What will you achieve in the first 30 days, the next 30 days, and the final 30 days?

This may be a good opportunity to use an Agile methodology. We review this in detail in Chapter 16. However, you want to organize the plan into small, multidisciplinary teams, including sales and marketing. Have short, frequent stand-up meetings (at least weekly) to discuss your progress. Keep breaking down the activities into manageable tasks. Do not let perfect be the enemy of good enough. Get as much done as you can in the 90 days.

You should also have a steering committee. This will include key executives who are not involved in the project but have a stake in the success of your ABM mission and a stake in the business you are piloting ABM with. We suggest you meet with them at the outset, every 30 days along the way, and at the end. Their support is critical to moving from pilot to full ABM implementation.

You will want to be crystal clear with the steering committee about your goals and how you will measure success. Get their buy-in on the risks and challenges.

Create a simple and easily updatable dashboard that will allow the ABM pilot team and the steering committee to know how you are progressing. Be disciplined about updating this. Even if your pilot fails, you will want to convey that you are disciplined in your approach and have been learning and adjusting throughout the pilot in real time based on results.

Pilot Examples

In Chapter 6, we provide three examples of ABM campaigns. To help get you started, here are the three examples of pilots that have been implemented with our clients.

1:1 ABM Pilot

Company A has long-term agreements with around 30 major financial services firms. They were looking for ways to cross-sell additional services. Company A ran a pilot using intent data to identify who was in the market for these additional services. By switching on intent data, they immediately identified that three of their largest customers were showing high interest in it. But these customers were unaware that Company A even offered this service. The account manager identified the right person for the customer to speak with. After the account manager explained their capabilities, the customer agreed to add them to their RFP.

Company A's SDR team implemented this technique across 30 major accounts. They integrated intent data from ZoomInfo into Salesforce. The SDRs now start their daily prospecting routines by focusing on the high-intent accounts.

1:Few ABM Pilot

This type involves targeting prospects with something in common. For example, Company B has a technology-enabled service that is especially useful to customers that use a certain ERP platform. Company B determined that new customers that had most recently adopted this ERP platform had a higher need for their solution. They also identified that customers that adopted this ERP platform typically realized this issue was problematic only a year after switching.

Company B developed an ABM campaign targeting about 100 accounts known to have switched ERP platforms in the last three years. This included a list of about 1,000 contacts across these accounts representing the typical buyer collective. These accounts were targeted with LinkedIn and email sequences using messages, content, and other tactics tailored to problems these accounts encountered.

1:Many ABM Pilot

You can test out hypotheses about 1:Many ABM in simple ways, such as LinkedIn ads. For example, Company C ran a multivariate test using LinkedIn ads. In this test, Company C promoted multiple solutions across 650 accounts.

They set a baseline in the first three weeks by running ads on LinkedIn to a defined buyer collective across the 650 accounts. In weeks four through six, Company C narrowed the TAL to only those that were showing intent. They used third-party intent data from ZoomInfo. Ad performance increased when they refined the target to only those with intent signals. They found that over the three weeks, engagement with these ads increased by 50%.

• • •

We hope this chapter gives you what you need to get started and experimenting. In the next chapter, we review how to approach your plan to move from Crawl to Walk as you accelerate from experimentation to making ABM and Total Customer Growth part of how you operate.

Go to https://learn.totalcustomergrowth.com to access resources for this chapter including templates to help you design an ABM pilot.

CHAPTER 15

Scaling and Evolving

What You Will Learn in This Chapter

- How to assess how prepared your organization is to scale
- How to develop a strategic playbook
- The different models you can use, ranging from a low-cost model using limited additional technology to a high-investment model using a sophisticated ABM platform
- Staffing changes to consider

So, you have run a successful pilot, and your executive team has bought into the potential of ABM and the Total Customer Growth Model. Now, it is time to start scaling. It is time to move from crawling to walking.

This chapter is primarily about how you scale your operations to be better at Identifying Intent, Engaging, and Converting. However, the information can also be effectively applied to how you Grow existing customers.

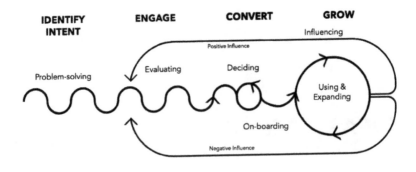

Readiness Assessment

Before you take off, it is good to take stock of where you are. In our work with clients, we use a tool called the "readiness assessment." This is a series of areas you should review before you start scaling.

The assessment covers three areas: foundations, planning, and execution. These include an assessment of your goals, ICPs, buyer journeys, content, engagement plan, data, team, project planning, and logistical considerations. The assessment allows you to evaluate your strengths, weaknesses, and gaps.

You can download an assessment template at learn.totalcustomergrowth.com.

ABM Playbook

The next step is to develop your strategy. We call this the "ABM playbook." If you have run a pilot as described in Chapter 14, you will have already produced your first ABM playbook.

The ABM playbook is a detailed and comprehensive strategic plan for using ABM and ABX to achieve your goals. Many of our clients use the ABM playbook as their marketing strategy. Period.

The ABM playbook includes:

Goals and Business Dynamics

- Clearly defined, measurable goals, including what you aim to achieve each quarter
- A description of the challenges and barriers you face, both external and internal
- Opportunities you can capitalize on now or in the coming months

Customers and Buyer Journeys

- Create a clear definition of your ICPs and the characteristics of a best-fit customer. See Chapter 4.
- Map out the buyer collectives for your ICPs, identifying champions, influencers, and decision-makers.
- Understand the personas and buyer journeys for your champions; it is valuable to do the same for some of the influencers and decision-makers. See Chapter 5.
- Create a priority list of the most important issues and questions that need to be addressed in the buyer journey. We suggest a top-ten list.

Content and Engagement Strategy

- Using this priority list, create your content strategy, including a list of topics, content types, and short abstracts for the first 90 days of content. See Chapter 6.

- Create an engagement plan that lays out the tactics you will use across the buyer journey to engage the champion personas.
- Identify how you will use 1:1, 1:Few, and 1:Many strategies and where intent data fits into your plans. You will also want to consider what your SDRs will focus on in the next three months. See Chapters 8 and 9.

Detailed Planning

- Using the content and engagement plans, create a detailed calendar and project plan for the first 90 days. You will repeat these every 90 days.
- Create a budget and resource plan for the next 12 months.

Measurement

- Lastly, outline how you will measure this and what your KPI dashboard will include. See Chapter 10.

Creating the ABM Playbook

We found that the best way to develop the playbook is through a series of collaborative strategy sessions. To do this, you will want to assemble a group of marketing, sales, and, ideally, customer success team members who know the customers and the primary business issues they face. You should have people who understand the various tactics you will employ as part of the playbook.

When we help clients develop their ABM playbook, we prefer weekly meetings that iteratively build out the strategy. Here is a typical schedule:

Week 1 - One 90-minute meeting: goal-setting, business dynamics, ICPs, best-fit customers, and buyer collectives

Week 2 - Two 90-minute meetings: defining personas and completing the buyer journeys for the champions, at minimum

Week 3 - One 90-minute meeting: content brainstorming and prioritization

Week 4 - One 90-minute meeting: engagement tactics discussion and engagement plan creation

Week 5 - One 90-minute meeting: reviewing detailed plan, budget, operations, and 90-day calendar

Each of these sessions requires a facilitator and a scribe to stimulate discussion and ensure that the ideas, insights, recommendations, and agreements are captured. As you can imagine, considerable work must be done between sessions to document and refine the outcomes of these sessions.

It is an enjoyable, worthwhile process and invariably leads to bigger, better ideas than doing it solo. None of us is as smart as all of us!

You can get templates to use in each of these sessions at learn.totalcustomergrowth.com.

Evolving

When you look at the customer list and ABM case studies provided by the leading ABM platform firms, it would be easy to conclude that

ABM is only for companies with deep pockets. It is true that implementing one of these platforms requires budgets upward of $100,000 for software licenses, implementation fees, and ad spends on ABM. However, ABM does not have to be that expensive.

You can tailor ABM to your business, regardless of your size. The basic principles of ABM are as relevant to a sole-practitioner B2B firm as they are to a Fortune 500 company. The key is to be disciplined in deciding which accounts you will pursue, focusing on the buyers, understanding how they decide to hire vendors, and taking a personalized approach in how you engage them.

Here are three different ABM scenarios that show how you can employ ABM principles at different budget levels.

The Low-Cost Model

Can you implement ABM with a limited tech stack?

Yes!

But the process is manual and can be a grind.

In the previous chapter, we provide three examples of ABM pilots. Each one of these was implemented without an ABM platform or a sophisticated marketing automation system.

Here are some examples of tools that are available for those with limited budgets:

LinkedIn Sales Navigator

For about $100 per month per seat, LinkedIn Sales Navigator is a valuable and very cost-effective tool for the budget-conscious ABM practitioner. It allows you to create a list of your target accounts, a list of contacts by accounts, and lists that allow you to track accounts that are engaging with you. LinkedIn Sales Navigator now includes second-party intent data that will pinpoint which prospects and accounts are engaging with your content and social media posts on LinkedIn.

You can also use Sales Navigator as an outreach to prospects, using DM and InMail. It can be a simple, effective way to run outreach sequences.

Leadfeeder and LeadLander

One of the biggest challenges is knowing who is engaging with you. These two low-cost tools can help with this. They provide you with insights about which accounts are engaging on your website and what they are looking at. This knowledge enhances your first-party intent data. They are not perfect, as they depend heavily on IP addresses for this information, so they provide data on only a partial list of the accounts on your website.

Third-Party Intent Data

You do not have to buy an ABM platform like Demandbase, Terminus, or 6sense to use third-party intent data. You can buy this directly from vendors like Bombora and ZoomInfo and directly see who is showing intent for topics that are relevant to you. This will be a big investment for a small firm, however, because annual licenses are in the tens of thousands of dollars. However, if you are committed to an ABM strategy, this can be invaluable. You can initially leverage a free (limited) trial of some of these intent solutions, like Bombora, to see the weekly top ten accounts showing intent for topics that are relevant to you. If you have not used these tools before, we recommend giving this a try and seeing how this data can provide insights to deliver targeted outreach before you make the investment.

Low-Cost Marketing Automation

You will need a marketing automation system to run automated campaigns. There are many CRM and marketing automation systems to choose from. For example, Ontraport is a simple platform that has many of the features that platforms like HubSpot, Pardot, and Marketo have, but at a fraction of the license fee.

NetLine

When it comes to running content marketing campaigns, NetLine is worth considering. This is a syndication network that will generate leads with target accounts using gated content. As you pay only for the leads you get, it can be very cost-efficient.

LinkedIn Ads

We love that LinkedIn lets you run ads to specific titles at a defined set of accounts. And as we describe in the third pilot example in the previous chapter, you can overlay intent data to make your ads work even harder.

B2B Media Companies

Many of the major media firms, such as HIMSS Media and TechTarget in health care technology, now offer ABM programs that include intent data, engagement dashboards, and highly targeted ABM campaigns.

Upwork, Fiverr, and Freelancer

These freelancer platforms are amazing resources for finding talent who can help you with implementation. We have used these to outsource LinkedIn outreach programs, and we find brilliant content writers, strategists, and even animators to create videos.

Google Sheets Dashboards

Our final low-cost favorite (or in this case, free favorite) is Google Sheets. This spreadsheet system can be used to create simple, easily shareable, and easy-to-update dashboards.

The Moderate-Cost Model

You can also implement ABM at greater scale if you have a more sophisticated marketing automation platform, such as HubSpot, Pardot, or Marketo.

Platforms like HubSpot were traditionally designed for outbound marketing and marketing to individuals rather than accounts. However, they have adapted and now have functionality that allows you to take an ABM approach.

If you are using HubSpot, let's look at how you can adapt it to an ABM approach. We want to give a special thank-you to Enoch Pakanati and his team at The Smarketers for their insights in this area.

HubSpot has three key properties that facilitate ABM activities. Data from these three properties is leveraged by ABM reports, lists, dashboards, target accounts, and account overview.

Target Account

Target account is a company property that allows companies to get a high-level, bird's-eye view of progress across all target accounts, including the number of target accounts, open deal value, accounts with open deals, and missing buyer roles.

Buying Role

A new contact property, buying role identifies the role that a stakeholder plays in the sales process. A contact may have more than one role or share a similar role with another contact. Missing buying roles makes ABM difficult to implement, as companies cannot practice hyper-focused marketing without adequate information on the role of each player in the sales process.

ICP Tiers

The ICP tier is a property that classifies companies based on how closely they meet your ICP criteria. For example, companies categorized in tier 1 are a great fit for your product, those in tier 2 only slightly meet your criteria, and companies in tier 3 are considered lower priority.

HubSpot's ABM Workflows

Using HubSpot's workflows for ABMs, you can customize and create templates for many processes in the sales cycle, including ideal company profile tier setting, lead nurturing, and account and sales notifications. While the ICP workflow makes ICP tiering less cumbersome, automated lead nurturing, as it is named, nurtures leads until they are ready to engage with sales. Account and sales notifications will notify teams based on ABM activity, like buying role conversions and target account activity.

HubSpot Integrations with ABM Tools

While HubSpot integrates with various ABM tools, three of the most popular integrations are as follows:

- **Bombora and ZoomInfo intent data** - Import third-party intent data directly into HubSpot and show intent signals by account.
- **LinkedIn** - By connecting LinkedIn ads to HubSpot, B2B marketers can create a company audience list to automatically sync companies from target accounts to the matched audience in LinkedIn.
- **Slack** - HubSpot and Slack integration offer certain functionalities that help execute an ABM strategy. Some of these include creating deal- or company-based Slack channels, sharing notes in HubSpot to Slack during a call or meeting, and turning Slack conversations into tasks within HubSpot.

ABM Reporting on HubSpot

HubSpot lets companies track the progress of their ABM campaigns through the following options:

- **Account-Based Marketing Dashboard** - Designed for the marketing department, this dashboard highlights the most engaged customers and reports the number of accounts in each ICP tier and how many times a target account has visited the organization's website.

- **My Target Accounts** - This dashboard keeps track of TALs, including recently closed accounts, the last sales activity, and the most recent engagement from target accounts.
- **Target Account Landscape** - This dashboard gives sales and marketing directors a high-level overview of target accounts and includes the number of target accounts by industry and associated contacts, as well as how many web pages were viewed by each account.

Here is how to get started with an ABM campaign:

1. Look up all companies in your CRM. Click on **More Filters** and select the Target Account property.
2. Filter accounts by annual revenue, industry, number of employees, etc., depending on the company's product or service.
3. Select all these accounts and add them to a static list.
4. Send specific and personalized marketing messages (blogs, emails, white papers, etc.). These can solve a specific and/or unique problem for the accounts in the same list.
5. Create a workflow that best suits the content created and industry specifications.
6. Start small. If you find success, base future campaigns on the original workflow.

The Fully Scaled ABM Model

As you gain confidence using ABM, and the results justify continued investment, you will need to take a big step up in several areas: technology, staffing, customer insight, and influencer marketing.

Technology

The biggest step change will be in your tech stack. We know of organizations using ABM at scale that have 60-plus tools in their tech stack. There is good justification for this number. As you grow your ABM capability, you will need to automate more and increasingly sophisticated marketing workflows. These are too complex and labor-intensive to do without automation.

Some more advanced ABM organizations split their budgets: a third on staff, a third on program dollars, and a third on tech stack. The tough thing to explain to your management is that spending several hundred thousand dollars on additional software will save you from having to spend more in the other two areas. Done well, your tech stack enables a much more efficient marketing model.

There is a perception that ABM is just about buying new toys for marketing. This is false. The challenge however, is convincing management that ABM is as strategically important and operationally critical as an ERP, workforce, or payroll system.

Here are some of the components of a fully capable ABM tech stack:

- **Intent data (e.g., Bombora and ZoomInfo)** - When you purchase an ABM platform, it will come with intent data. We believe it is also worth purchasing third-party intent data separately. This is because you will want your sales and SDR teams to have direct access to it. The best way to do this is to integrate it directly into the CRM (i.e., where SDRs do their work). Note: You will not be entirely successful if you expect sales and SDR team members to access this in the ABM platform. They simply will not use it unless it is seamlessly part of their workflow.

- **The ABM platform** - The various ABM platforms (Terminus, Demandbase, 6sense, RollWorks, Triblio) have many similarities. Each has its own pros and cons, but at their hearts, they are ABM workflow engines. They are designed to automate the way you interact with prospects across the buyer journey in a more intelligent and efficient way. They make it simple for you to react automatically to changes in buyer behavior so that when a buyer signals intent, they can be presented with ads, content, and messages that address where they are in the buyer journey and what their specific issues are at that time. These platforms are designed to help you deliver the right message to the right buyer at the right time. They also make it easy for you to track buyers moving through your pipeline and respond intelligently to accelerate through to a conversion. Currently, this cannot be done with a CRM or marketing automation system.

- **Enterprise-grade CRM** - This is the system of record for sales. This book does not set out to educate you about CRM and sales management, but simply put, you cannot operate at scale without one. Integrating your CRM with your ABM platform is a must-do, as it is essential in creating a seamless working relationship between sales and marketing.

- **Marketing automation system** - Your ABM platform can automate many of the aspects of marketing, such as ad targeting. However, it does not currently do all that you need in terms of marketing automation. You will need a system like Marketo, Eloqua, Salesforce, Pardot, or possibly HubSpot to run automated email and social media at the required scale and frequency.

- **Personalization tools** - As you know, personalization is a key principle of ABM. Your ABM platform provides some level of personalization in what messages are delivered to whom and at what time. There are additional tools to consider for your SDRs. For example, Uberflip makes it easy for your sales and SDR team to create personalized 1:1 landing pages on the fly. There is also a tool in Terminus (the tool was formerly known as Sigstr) that embeds a targeted ad banner in your email signature. This allows you to advertise specific messages to different buyers in your email.

- **Media channels** - Most ABM platforms include a demand-side ad platform that allows you to run hyper-targeted display ads across the internet. You can also use these platforms to run ads across other digital channels, such as streaming services on TV (like Hulu) or streaming apps (like Spotify). Using alternative channels creates an opportunity to break through the clutter of websites and reach buyers in ways that cut through the noise.

Staffing

The second area where you will need to invest more is staffing. There are two roles that will become essential to run Total Customer Growth at scale:

- **ABM manager** - You will need to have someone on the team whose full-time job is ABM. They will be the subject-matter expert on ABM and be responsible for campaign strategy, ensuring that campaign parameters are set up appropriately in your ABM platform; another function will be to work with the rest of the team to educate and assist with ABM campaigns. They should also be on the cutting edge of tools and techniques to evaluate. Early on in your ABM evolution, these responsibilities may be part of someone's job, but as you grow your ABM capabilities, it will become evident that you need someone in a full-time role.

- **Marketing operations** - This person is like Scotty in *Star Trek*. They run the engine room of your ABM system. They oversee the ABM platform, marketing automation system, data management, and integration with other systems, like the CRM. They work in concert with sales operations. In some firms, marketing operations is part of sales operations. These people are also responsible for creating dashboards and the reports needed to keep ABM programs moving.

ABM increases the need for content. So, in addition to these roles, you should expect to scale up your specialist roles, such as content writers, designers, video producers, and social media experts.

Advanced Total Customer Growth Capabilities

In Part 3, we review ABX capabilities that, combined with a full-stack ABM engine, create a Total Customer Growth Model.

You can add these capabilities at any stage. Still, it is not unusual for an organization to regard this as the natural next step after implementing a fully scaled-up ABM engine. Two major evolutions will convert your ABM engine into a Total Customer Growth Model:

- **Account insights** - As we review in Chapter 12, account insights is fundamental to Total Customer Growth. Using tools like NPS is a good start, but many have limitations, especially in complex sales. In Chapter 12, we review in detail how to gain better account insights and use this to grow your existing customers.

- **Influencer marketing** - One of the keys to a Total Customer Growth Model is turning positively disposed customers into evangelists. It can also require neutralizing negative customers. In Chapter 13, we explain how to do this. The key strategy here is called "influencer marketing." This is a complex marketing discipline that involves listening to social media, creating customer champions, and having procedures in place to rapidly address concerns from negative customers.

● ● ●

In the next chapter, we take a diversion to discuss how to make your marketing operations more Agile. Agile marketing is fast becoming an effective operating model. We believe it is a highly effective way to evolve, scale, and operate a Total Customer Growth Model.

So, let's get Agile!

Go to https://learn.totalcustomergrowth.com to access resources for this chapter including the Total Customer Growth Planning Framework.

CHAPTER 16

Being Agile

What You Will Learn in This Chapter

- What Agile marketing is and why it is important
- Why adopt Agile marketing and how to start the process
- How Agile marketing works in practice
- What best practice in Agile marketing is
- How Agile changes the way your marketing teams operate
- What is critical to success and how to manage the transformation

Agile marketing has received a great deal of attention. For many organizations, it is becoming *the* operating model for marketing.

Marketing executives, like Kaycee Kalpin, CMO of Premier, Inc., have adopted Agile marketing. Kaycee led the transformation of a team of more than 50 marketers to this new model.

In this chapter, we share what Agile marketing is and how it was implemented at Premier.

So, What Is Agile Marketing?

According to Atlassian, a major software firm staffed by masters in Agile:

> Agile Marketing is **an approach to marketing that utilizes the principles and practices of agile methodologies.** This includes having self-organizing, cross-functional teams doing work in frequent iterations with continuous feedback.

Agile marketing is no different from Agile practices in other areas, including software development. It is doing more with less. It is a way to carve out a body of work, put a timeline to it, and create a cross-functional team to get the work done in a time-efficient and time-boxed way.

Why Make the Change to Agile Marketing?

There are many reasons to consider changing to Agile marketing. These include:

- Budgets are being cut or are not growing.
- Campaigns are not delivering sufficient results to justify the spending on marketing.
- It is taking too long to complete projects and tasks.
- Increasing the team size is not improving business outcomes.

In Kaycee's situation, it was driven by the need to adapt to frequent changes in organizational structure. She found a great deal of inefficiency in the handoff from one vertical to the next, no matter how they were aligned. The goal was to make the team more adaptive.

How Agile Marketing Works in Practice

Let's say there is a gap in the pipeline, and marketing needs to launch a campaign that quickly increases deal flow. The goal might be to get sales five opportunities within 30 days.

First, you do a brainstorming session. You put down everything possible that you could do in a campaign to achieve the goal. Then, you assign points based on the level of effort required. Different organizations use different point structures. Kaycee's team used the number of hours it took to complete this task.

For example, if someone comes up with a webinar, there needs to be an invite, a registration page, an invitation, a list pulled, a webinar executed, polls within the webinar, and content. That is a high number of points.

Then, you put all your ideas up on the board and rank them in terms of the level of effort and leads that each would generate. You go back to the board with the team and ask, "What can we reasonably accomplish in a two-week sprint that gets us to the lead number goal?"

That point system helps you determine a reasonable amount of work that this team can do to get those five opportunities. Your tactics may shift around a little. Maybe a webinar is not the best way to do it because it will take three weeks to get it to market. Maybe you do an on-demand webinar with a prior event instead.

How to Teach Agile Marketing to the Team

Before the pandemic (and not knowing the pandemic was coming), Kaycee had a consultant teach her team the principles of Agile.

The coach had them make pizzas out of construction paper. Someone was cutting the construction paper, someone was coloring the construction paper, and someone was taping the pepperonis onto the pizza. Essentially, this created an assembly line. As the teams assessed the process, they noticed where things got held up. For example, they needed more scissors. The process was getting held up at the stage of cutting the pizza because someone was being too meticulous with their scissors work. This exercise taught the team to shift their mindset to look holistically at the work being done and the goal they were trying to meet. Understanding this enabled teams to create a line of individuals and resources to get there, regardless of functional alignment, skill set, or job description.

How Agile Marketing Changes the Way Teams Work

One of Kaycee's key recommendations is to avoid reorganizing the department. At Premier, people kept the same titles, and the org chart remained largely unchanged. The most important thing was changing how they worked.

In practice, you measure the team's output. That's hard sometimes, as it identifies weak links in creating Agile teams with a project owner, called a "scrum master." No one on the team, or very few on the Agile team, reported to that person. The coaching and development of the person happened in their vertical. For example, a digital analyst is coached by someone specializing in digital, but they may be attached to a team working on a project.

The team did daily stand-ups and reported what they did in the previous 24 hours. Everybody chipped in, and the peer-to-peer interaction held people accountable, helping to improve team productivity.

One of the critical benefits during the pandemic was that Agile kept people very connected.

To remain focused, you need the right tools. Premier started with a technology that did not work. They ripped it out and put in new project management software that they now use for sprints. You will need everybody to speak the same technical language. Everyone commits to the stand-up, whether it is weekly, daily, or biweekly. In a remote, virtual situation, Kaycee was a die-hard on using cameras so people looked at each other. They started with an icebreaker and then dove right in.

How Agile Marketing Changes Roles in the Marketing Department

Kaycee has a growth team that creates the campaigns and execution verticals (automation, digital, PR). She forms cross-functional teams.

One key learning from this transformation is that 100% specialization is the death of a marketing team with limited resources. For example, Kaycee's team has a tight marketing budget, so someone exclusively dedicated to LinkedIn is deployed at 40%.

When you all specialize, you are telling someone that they operate in a specific box and cannot color outside the box. This limits their productivity, contribution, and development. It also limits the collective potential of the whole marketing team, especially if you have omnichannel.

It can be especially hard for people who are perfectionists. Agile can put a strain on creative specialists. They want to deliver a 10 out of 10 in terms of effort every time. They want to create the best digital ad they have ever seen. But you may need only a 3 out of 10 because you need 10 digital ads. So, when you tell someone who specializes in something that you need a 3, they are not going to be happy with the work they deliver. But if you tell a team that you need to do this ten times to try, they start to get it.

Success Factors

Critical to Success #1 – Working Toward Specific Goals

You are working toward a specific goal. So, the key is making the team think differently about how they achieve these goals. For example, how often do you have people come to you and say, "We're running a campaign. It's a webinar"? And you reset their thinking by responding, "A webinar isn't a campaign." Thought leadership that leads to a webinar that leads to a telemarketing call that converts to a sales meeting is a campaign. And so, it helps people think differently about what they are working toward.

This can improve the way you approach annual planning. Typically, the annual plan can be the death of everyone because, on paper, it looks as if it is going to work. When you start deploying tactics that are not working, you generally persist with things that do not work. Kaycee's approach is to break down the work into campaigns that contribute to growth in three business areas. Then, they break down that work into two-week sprints. For example, she might say, "This week, we're going to work on this slice of the market, or these two weeks, we're going to work on this slice of the market, and we're going to try to increase engagement in two weeks of these ten accounts by 2%." The critical thing is to break down the work to the slightest degree that provides an impact.

Critical to Success #2 - Top Down

It has to start from the top down. You must align from the CMO down, and the CEO must be on board because as the CMO, you will have to say no to things. And the early stages are the hardest because you have to report more and overcommunicate. For example, "This is what the team is doing in this two-week sprint, here is what we accomplished, and here is how it was measured." Kayce said they went through ten two-week sprints before they started to get buy-in from some of the P&L owners. She got the CEO to say a few things about it at meetings and talk about how marketing was trained in Agile, that they were rolling out these new principles, and patience was needed.

How to Manage the Team through the Transformation to Agile

The pandemic created an inflection point to transform to Agile. When the pandemic started, the executive team shifted their philosophy from selling hard to supporting their customers. Premier, Inc., serves 5,000 health systems, and especially during the height of the pandemic, those health systems did not want to be sold to. So, Kaycee and her colleagues focused on communicating with them about what resources Premier could offer to help them through their journey.

As an Agile team, they needed to be fully committed to this strategy. Kaycee took a 60/40 approach, where they spent 60% of their time on the deliverables through Agile, and 40% on business as usual. The team found that the Agile projects drove them more, as they were more rewarding. They were working as a team, coloring outside the lines, and finishing projects that had a goal attached to the organization's goals in sprints. They were even more productive in the 60% of projects done through Agile.

Challenges That Arise Out of This Transformation

One of the biggest challenges with Agile is in the war for talent.

As an organization, you are going to get more done for less money, and you are going to get better results, but people management can be challenging.

Staff turnover is a significant issue for everyone. The problem is convincing individuals that there is a development path. As they are part of a unit where everyone is equal, no one has more power. And if they win, they all win. But if they fail, they all fail.

The problem is that individuals struggle to see how they can climb the corporate ladder. How do they go from manager to director to vice president to CMO? And how do they maintain a semblance of specialization?

Key Takeaways

- Agile marketing is about doing more with less and creating cross-functional teams to get the work done in a time-efficient and time-boxed way.
- There are many reasons to adopt Agile marketing. At the end of the day, it can change up your team's productivity and improve results.
- Avoid a reorganization of the department. Do not change people's titles or the org chart. The most important thing is to change how the team works.

- Avoid specialization and encourage team members to color outside the lines.

- Ensure you have marketing project management software that works for your organization.

- Agile marketing starts with a focus on a specific goal. Being more goal-focused is one of the key changes.

- You kick off an Agile marketing project by brainstorming ideas, breaking those ideas into many small tasks, then scoring and ranking the ideas based on the level of effort and potential results.

- The next step is to design a series of short sprints with a cross-functional team assigned to each sprint, managed by a scrum master.

- One of the key elements of Agile marketing is regular (often daily) stand-ups—meetings in which all the team members report on progress. This knowledge allows the team to adjust as needed and quickly.

- You will also change what you measure. You become even more focused on productivity and outcomes.

- You most likely need to bring in a specialist coach to teach the team how to implement Agile marketing practices. This includes having many team members become certified in Agile.

- Many tools support Agile marketing. These include project management tools, like Tenon, Monday.com, and Asana

- Getting executive buy-in is critical. You will need the CEO's support as you transition to effective and fully functioning Agile marketing capability.

- One of the hardest adjustments is that a 10 out of 10 in quality is not always needed. Sometimes 3 out of 10 is sufficient.

- One of the biggest issues people have in an Agile marketing environment is the concern about how their careers will advance.

> Go to https://learn.totalcustomergrowth.com to access resources for this chapter including an interview with Kaycee Kalpin on how she built an Agile marketing team.

CHAPTER 17

The Total Customer Growth Organization

What You Will Learn in This Chapter

- What Total Customer Growth looks like at scale
- What impact that will have on an organization
- The seven skills you will need to move your organization toward Total Customer Growth

We have broken down the steps and components to build a Total Customer Growth Model. Right now, it might feel like we have given you a car that is still in kit form. In this final chapter, we paint a picture of what this might look like when you are in the Run stage, and Total Customer Growth, ABM, and ABX are part of the fabric of how you operate.

This chapter is about envisioning the Total Customer Growth Model in action, at scale.

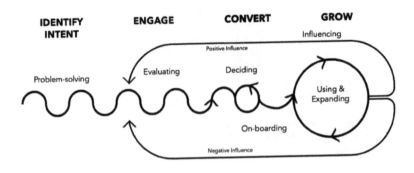

A Total Customer Growth Scenario

Let's imagine that you are the CMO of an enterprise software company that sells security solutions to the financial services market. You have six people on the marketing team, and you partner with the CRO, who has a dozen salespeople. In addition, there are six SDRs who now report to you. The customer success team has seven managers, one of whom is closely connected with marketing.

It is early in the year, and you have a revenue goal to add ten new customers and $20 million in net new revenue. You also need to help ensure that customer churn does not drop below 10%.

As you start the year, there is gap in the pipeline needed to achieve the goals for the year. Given that sales cycles are six to nine months, it is critical that you expand the opportunity pipeline.

In partnership with sales and the SDR teams, you need to add ten new qualified opportunities to the pipeline each quarter.

In addition, your recent customer satisfaction survey is a little troubling, as 30% of your customers have a renewal coming up this year, and about half of these accounts have given neutral or negative reviews. This is a big hill to climb.

What follows is how you attack these goals and find buyers with intent for your solutions, engage them, convert some of them, and move them to a decision. Then, as they become customers, how you will help on-board them, upsell them, and turn them into evangelists.

Intent

Finding Buyers Defining a Problem

You kick off the year by assembling a team to identify a pipeline of net new prospects. This includes three members of your marketing team (including revops), three SDRs, two sales managers, and a customer success team member.

At the end of the year, new legislation will be introduced that could increase demand for the category of software you sell. You have a dozen competitors, and while you are well-regarded, awareness is still low relative to others in your category. Your company would not automatically get on the list of vendors to be considered.

As a team, you agree that you need to focus on accounts that appear to be researching the cybersecurity issues related to the upcoming legislation.

Given that you need to get results in a short time frame, the team brainstorms different tactics and content you could use to find in-market prospects. Using your Agile scoring methodology, your marketing team proposes the following:

- Using new intent topics that are relevant to the upcoming legislation and cybersecurity topics
- Running an educational webinar featuring a customer and your head of product development
- Creating a short series of educational blog posts on the cyber-security issues related to the upcoming legislation

- Launching an ad campaign targeting accounts showing intent
- Providing a sales sheet to the SDRs with new sales messaging

Getting Quick Customer Insight

The marketing team starts developing these tactics. You and the customer success team member meet with three or four customers to get their insights on how the new legislation will affect them. You also ask customer success to recommend a customer who could speak at the webinar.

After you speak with the customers, it is clear that there are five key issues that concern buyers about the new legislation. In addition, one of the sales reps has attended a customer discussion on this topic, and he validates that these issues are the top priorities. You brief the team to develop content about these issues.

You instruct a marketing team member to update the buyer journey with this new information.

As this is going on, one of the marketing team members, the revops manager, and two of the SDRs set up a campaign plan in the ABM platform. The first thing they do is create a new set of intent clusters and run a report against the TAL and the current customer list.

They see that 30% of the TAL and 25% of current accounts are spiking for these intent topics. They also notice that many of the at-risk customers that may defect are also spiking. The customer success manager is notified, and it is agreed that these customers will be personally invited to the webinar.

The customer success manager says his team will also ensure that all the new content is personally sent to these at-risk customers.

Targeting New In-Market Prospects

You start rolling out the campaign using your ABM platform as the command center. Your marketing team runs display and LinkedIn ads to accounts showing intent, inviting them to attend the webinar. In addition, you run an email campaign to all customers and target accounts.

As blog posts are produced, you publish them as posts in your LinkedIn campaign targeting accounts showing intent. Webinar registrants receive the blog posts via email.

In parallel, the SDRs personally invite prospects that are already in the pipeline to attend the webinar, and customer success does the same with existing customers.

Senior executives are alerted about the at-risk accounts, and you request that they invite these accounts to attend the webinar as well.

The webinar runs at the start of month three and is well attended. There are 300 registrants, and 100 attended the webinar. The SDRs are in active follow-up mode with registrants.

Throughout the quarter, the SDRs have been calling into accounts showing intent and are able to secure 20 initial meetings. Out of these, six prospects convert into sales-qualified opportunities, and sales takes over moving them through the sales pipeline.

Within the first 90 days, 100 new accounts have engaged with these marketing activities and seem to be actively engaged in gaining a better understanding of the issues related to the new legislation.

Engage

How to Help the Buyer Solve Their Problem

As the campaign progresses, it becomes apparent based on the engagement metrics in the ABM platform that certain pieces of content perform better than others. In addition, the post-webinar survey gives strong indications on what additional information buyers are interested in.

The marketing team takes the lead in developing new content geared more toward helping buyers understand the different options to address the new legislation. They start creating a long-form written guide.

In a weekly team meeting, one of the SDRs suggests that short videos would be effective in converting the pipeline. Marketing asks the head of product marketing to create two or three short videos about how to solve the challenges related to the new legislation.

Getting Prospects to Put Their Hands Up

Meanwhile, the SDRs are focusing their attention on moving 100 actively engaged accounts to schedule a call. They have been sending a customized email sequence to five to ten contacts at each account. In addition, they create personalized pages for some of these accounts that curate the new solution-oriented content and house the new videos.

Over the next 30 days, 30 out of the 100 actively engaged accounts visit the personalized pages multiple times and read three or four pieces of content. The SDRs redouble their efforts and are able to secure 15 additional meetings. Most of these accounts are interested in further discussion and transition to sales. Ten become sales-qualified opportunities, meeting the quarterly goal.

In parallel, the ongoing educational campaign has surfaced another 150 accounts that are showing intent.

Current Customer Education

The customer success manager takes advantage of the new content and creates personalized pages for the at-risk customers. Engagement metrics show that most of these read the content and visit these pages multiple times.

Anecdotally, the customer success manager tells the team in the weekly meeting that many of the at-risk customers seem to be turning around. Some indicate that their concerns have been alleviated, and they may seem more likely to renew.

The Evaluation Stage

As a follow-up to the solution-oriented content, marketing creates several evaluation-oriented content pieces, including an RFP template and a buyer checklist. They run an intent-based campaign using competitor names as topics, as well the prior used topics. The ads have a conversion rate two times higher than baseline conversion rates.

This activity identifies another 50 new accounts that are showing interest in this subject area. Additionally, these tactics work well with the 250 already-identified accounts.

The SDRs are able to get additional meetings with 15 accounts. They also identify ten accounts where the CEO has a connection. The CRO asks the CEO to reach out to these accounts with a very specific message related to the new legislation. This action results in another five meetings.

Convert

As they enter second quarter, the team is pleased to have met their quarterly goal. It is agreed with sales to continue the campaign and aim to deliver at least ten new qualified opportunities per quarter.

Moving Deals

The pipeline of qualified opportunities is building, and the sales team is actively engaged in trying to convert these.

Working with marketing, the sales team sets a view in their CRM that shows other intent topics that these qualified-opportunity accounts are spiking for. They use these to share content via their LinkedIn profiles, which helps them expand their connections within each account.

They also have the CEO record a short video on her passion for this topic and send this via email and LinkedIn DM to the buyer collective contacts at each opportunity.

They also set up account-level alerts for each account to surface additional news and information that could be relevant in creating personalized messages.

Meanwhile, the marketing team updates the personalized pages for each opportunity to include relevant case studies and video testimonials.

While it is hard to tell at the time, when they analyze the closed deals later, they see that the sales cycles were 20% shorter than typical deals of a similar size.

Closing the Deals and Onboarding

The opportunities continue to move through the pipeline. Pricing is negotiated. The customer success team is introduced, and implementation guides are added to the personal pages. This includes best-practice blog posts on successful implementations.

As deals are signed and prospects become customers, customer success takes the lead. On-boarding begins with a personal introductory email from the CEO.

The customer success team has built an inventory of best practice guides and training videos that are part of the process of kicking off the relationship.

One of the key events during the on-boarding is creating a customer charter. This is an expectation-setting document that will be revisited periodically.

Grow

Usage and Expansion

In year one of the relationship with a new customer, customer success ensures that marketing includes the new customers in the biannual satisfaction study. Custom questions are added to reflect issues around the new legislation.

Customer success is happy to see that most of the new customers give the company high ratings, but they are concerned that two of the new customers are dissatisfied. One of these is a surprise. Customer success puts in place a mitigation plan.

Customer success notices that a new feature addresses one of the issues that comes up in many surveys. They realize that new features released six months prior were supposed to address this. The conclusion is that customers are unaware of the new functionality.

They team up with marketing to create a customer awareness campaign about the new functionality, which is successful and creates 20 upsell opportunities with existing customers.

Evangelizing Your Business

In partnership with marketing, customer success initiates a customer celebration program.

They start by identifying the most committed customers based on the most recent survey. Initially this includes several easy-to-execute tactics:

- Celebrating their wins by reposting and tagging when customers are featured in the press or social media
- Giving them advance notice when good news is about to break, such as winning an award, making a major hire, or closing a funding round
- Tagging customers in social media when the company posts something relevant about them

They plan an annual customer event that will celebrate customers and create a forum for them to tell their stories. The event will include key prospects, as well as at-risk customers, by creating a forum for senior executives to hear their concerns directly.

As a result of the first event, 20 customers agree to be references for future prospects, and 5 agree to be take part in creating case studies. This will include being featured in trade media and social media.

Following the event, customer success and marketing create a campaign for existing customers to rate them on Capterra and G2.

Marketing meets with customer success every two weeks to determine how this program can be further publicized in social media and PR.

Positive Impact in Summary

In this scenario, multiple departments work seamlessly toward common goals. They use customer insight and intent data to achieve those goals through campaigns tailored to in-market accounts.

Marketing feels they have more control in generating demand. They also appreciate that the sales, SDR, and customer success teams are more collaborative. SDRs and sales feel that the quality of the opportunities is improving. Deal sizes seem to be larger, deals are moving through the pipeline, and they can tell what is most or least effective in increasing the velocity of each deal.

As deals convert, customer success is better prepared, and they have the tools in place to on-board customers quickly. They also have better visibility into satisfaction issues and where they need to focus. Customer retention improves as a result.

The customer champion program further improves customer commitment and creates a pool of customer evangelists who will act on the firm's behalf to help them win more business.

Total Customer Growth Leadership Skills

If this vision is what you want to achieve, there are seven skills you will need to master.

1. Being a Change Agent

Total Customer Growth is an ambitious vision. It will require significant change. As we all know, change is hard. It will require courage and support from the C-suite, especially the CEO. You will need to take the long view in what you are trying to achieve and have short-term goals with success milestones every quarter. Take the vision described above and break down what you can achieve into quarterly increments. Look for wins every quarter that demonstrate progress and further cement buy-in.

2. Being Customer Driven

If we can convince you of one thing in this book, it is the importance of being customer driven. Many companies talk the talk about this, but very few are good at it. If you can be the expert in how your customers buy, what they need to hear and learn from you and when and how to read their signals, you will be successful in Total Customer Growth.

3. Fostering Collaboration

Simply put, without alignment among sales, SDRs, marketing, and customer success, your evolution toward Total Customer Growth will fail. You will need to be the one who makes collaboration happen. You will need to lead by example and model the behavior you are trying to engender.

4. Being Agile

Agile marketing is not a must-have, but it will help. By its nature, it is more efficient and fosters collaboration. You also need to create an environment that supports a team in reacting and responding to changes in behavior and new signals. You will need to motivate your team to work together to adapt and execute quickly.

5. A Passion for Experimentation

Build into your plans the time to test and try new things. Try something new every quarter, and use customer insights to inform new ideas. Be fearless in cutting activities that do not work as well and double down on new tactics that work. Both will help you accelerate change.

6. Mastering Measurement

This may the hardest thing to master, and it may also be the most important. If you can show how you are influencing the pipeline, strengthening customer relationships, and improving the way you grow profitable customers, change will follow.

7. Tenacity

Stick to it. You will be whipsawed by other priorities, and you will face resistance all the way. You will have to be stubborn in your vision and tenacious in driving the organization to change. If you do not make it happen, who will?

Every Journey Starts with a First Step

We hope that having read our book, you are ready to get started. There is no getting around it: Total Customer Growth is a big undertaking. It may take several years to make the transition completely.

So, how can you get started?

To help you take the first step, we have created four projects with instructions that you and your team can undertake in less than 90 days:

1. Write an ABM playbook: A step-by-step guide to creating your ABM playbook, with templates and videos
2. Use intent data with your SDRs: How to get your SDRs focused on in-market prospects
3. Create a simple intent-based ad campaign: Use intent data to identify in-market prospects and create a more targeted digital ad campaign via LinkedIn.
4. Future needs assessment: Gain a clear understanding about how you are positioned with key customers and pinpoint growth opportunities that you can turn into upsell opportunities.

> Go to https://learn.totalcustomergrowth.com to get instructions on how to implement these pilots.

Each of these will get you on your way.

ABM and ABX are evolving. And AI has the potential to transform them in radical ways. As more companies embrace it, we expect a new era of innovation in how companies like yours win and grow customers.

Although ABM has been around for a while, we believe we are still in the early stages of a revolution in B2B sales and marketing. Things are going to get even more exciting.

If you take one thing away from this book, know that a Total Customer Growth Model is a moat around your business. It will be very hard for your competitors to overcome the strength of your customer relationships and the effectiveness of your ABM-driven growth engine.

Equally, if you do not act and your competitors get ahead of you in embracing Total Customer Growth, it will be incredibly hard for you to beat them.

If you have not taken the first step on this journey, it is not too late. But if you wait it much longer, your competitors may just pass right by you.

Take the first step!

In closing, we hope this book has helped you envision a new future based on Total Customer Growth and shown you new ways of doing things.

We are always looking to improve what we do and how we do it. If there is anything we missed, that you do not understand, or that you disagree with, please let us know.

The best way to do that is to email adam.turinas@totalcustomer-growth.com.

We wish you great success in your journey toward Total Customer Growth.

Adam and Ben

EPILOGUE
Why We Wrote This Book

Adam's Story

When I was a teenager, all I wanted to do was go into advertising. It verged on an obsession.

My grandfather was a very successful and highly regarded UK ad guy in the 50s and 60s, so it was considered the family business. And I grew up in the UK in the 1970s—the heyday of British advertising, when the ads on TV were often more entertaining and more memorable than the shows.

Coming out of college, I was hired by the London office of Benton Bowles (which then became DMB&B) as a junior account executive. For three years, I worked on consumer-packaged goods and retail accounts, including General Foods, Tetley Tea, and Mars candy. It was an excellent apprenticeship. I even worked on the Wembley Stadium account. As a die-hard soccer fan, this was freakin' heaven.

Working for a big agency in London in the late '80s was about as fun as it gets. In the words of Jerry Della Femina, the famous NY ad guy, "I honestly believe that advertising is the most fun you can have with your clothes on."

He was spot on.

I moved to the US when I met Alice, the girl of my dreams, a Texan, who became my wife of thirty-four years. After I relocated, I joined the venerable Ogilvy & Mather. I was entering the University of Advertising. Ogilvy was where you learned how to do advertising the right way.

Working on Compaq (remember them?) and IBM, I learned how to market technology and about B2B marketing strategy and execution. And I learned better ways to develop brand strategy.

It was still fun, intellectually challenging, and frenetic, and it was pretty cool to tell my friends about.

But something was missing.

I had this nagging doubt. I wasn't entirely sure whether any of the advertising I was involved in worked.

We were creating famous ad campaigns. Our clients' sales were growing. But it did not seem to matter what we did and how we measured it—it was not ever really clear how our work made a difference.

We all passed this off with the famous quote attributed to John Wanamaker, the nineteenth-century retailer: "Half the money I spend on advertising is wasted; the trouble is I don't know which half."

We were asking clients to spend tens of millions of dollars on ad campaigns, and no matter how much we researched them and measured their impact, the cause and effect between what we produced and someone buying the product seemed tenuous.

Then, something changed for me.

In 1994, my father-in-law gave my family a PC for Christmas. This old 386-chip beige box came with a 9600 baud modem and a Netcom CD. I had never been online, and one evening, I thought I would give the new thing called the Worldwide Web a whirl. At six o'clock one night, I booted up the PC, put the Netcom disk in the CD drive, and got online for the first time. The hair stood up on the back of my neck. By three the next morning, I finally logged off. There were not many websites then, and by the time I went to bed, I had probably visited most of them. It was chaotic and hard to navigate. Most websites were corporate brochures, but it was clear that this was transformative.

I knew this could be the biggest thing in my career, and I wanted to get in early.

And what was clear at first sight was that this was a highly measurable medium. We would be able to attribute results to our efforts.

I jumped into the emerging digital industry very early and have never left it. For the next fifteen years, I worked in digital marketing. I loved how we could correlate our campaigns to results. It was not perfect, but it was so much better than the days before the web.

A little over ten years ago, I took a right turn. Through a series of random accidents, a physician friend and I started a health-tech company, Practice Unite (later renamed Uniphy Health).

We were focused on solving a big problem in health care: the terrible communications between clinicians. It is hard for doctors, nurses, and all the other professionals involved in caring for you and your loved ones to communicate with each other effectively and in a timely way. This challenge is a big part of patient safety issues. People die because of breakdowns in communications.

We developed an idea for a mobile app for clinicians. When we pitched this to the CEO of a hospital, he said, "You build it, and I'll buy it."

So, we did.

His hospital became our first of many customers. Users loved the app, and we were able to sell the solution to many other health care systems over the next few years. We eventually sold the business to a larger health-tech firm.

It was an exciting period in my life, but there was a big source of frustration.

As the CEO, I needed greater predictability in forecasting our sales. We suffered a few near-death experiences due to poor cash flow when deals did not convert or closed much later than expected. I endured a frequent battering from investors when we missed sales targets, which happened too often. And five years in, we had to lay off staff, as we were way off our growth forecasts.

It made me sick. I was desperate for a way to create and forecast demand in a more predictable way.

It was especially frustrating for me, as I had three decades of experience in marketing and selling B2B. Our marketing had generated demand, and we could see that our PR and social media were building awareness. In addition, demand-generation tactics would sporadically generate leads for our sales force. We also had some success in using LinkedIn to reach out and start new relationships.

The problem was that we had not developed a scalable way to build a forecastable sales pipeline.

When I started **health**launchpad in 2020, I had a double-edged mission. I wanted to help technology firms navigate health care more effectively. But my personal mission—my white whale—was to help companies develop more effective and more predictable ways of marketing.

When I met Ben, I knew a little about account-based marketing (ABM), but Ben's journey at Nuvolo opened my eyes to a better way of marketing.

Ben's Story

I grew up on a small 200-acre farm in southern Iowa with my parents and my brother and sister. I lived there from childhood through high school. My parents still farm today, even though they are retired now from their jobs—my dad as a civil engineer and my mom as a registered nurse.

When I got into the workforce during college, I started at an aerospace and defense company, Rockwell Collins, which is now Collins Aerospace. I worked in their IT department for about ten years, which helped me pay for my college education. As an IT technical support person, part of my job was fixing computer hardware and software that was broken or not operating properly.

One of the pieces of advice I always used when performing IT support was something my dad said: "Start from the known and work to the unknown."

This saying is ingrained in my mind, and I use it in about every unknown situation I run into in life, both personally and professionally.

When a tractor would break down while we were farming, we didn't have the luxury of just calling someone to come out to fix it. We had to fix it ourselves, and typically, we had serious pressure to get things back running that same day due to impending weather or crop conditions. This was when I would always hear my dad use the phrase "Start from the known," and we would figure out the issue and fix it when we could.

Now, let's fast forward to what got me into marketing. I ended up working for a startup SaaS software company, Nuvolo, after my role at Dell ended. At this startup, I was initially their lead solution consultant, then went on to build out their global pre-sales organization. In that role, I was one of their main presenters at trade shows, ran analyst relations with Gartner, and helped drive the overall messaging we used for marketing and selling.

Eventually, after about six years, I became their CMO and built out their overall marketing structure. I had a great team of marketing resources, including product marketing, corporate marketing, field marketing, and business development. When I started looking at the marketing function, I saw that it leveraged traditional marketing tactics focused on lead generation as the primary metric. These leads came from traditional marketing activities, like webinars, trade shows, social media, and digital advertising. The challenge with this model, though, was that we spent marketing dollars on items that were unproven or that we had a hard time measuring the direct return on investment.

This is when we decided to change how we marketed to an account-based model. We had a great set of marketing team members who drove this new strategy. This was not just a marketing approach. It was a whole-company approach. How we looked at prospective and existing customers changed. We were able to leverage real, known data to determine how we marketed and sold our solutions.

This book is designed to dive into the specifics of this new account-based approach for Total Customer Growth.

ACKNOWLEDGEMENTS

We first thank our families for your support, especially our wives, Alice Turinas and Montana Delk. You put up with the time it took us to get this completed. You listened patiently and (we think) attentively as we incessantly told you about every new chapter, every update, every piece of feedback.

We also want to thank all those who contributed ideas, case studies, quotes and insight that we hope we did justice to your input. A special thanks to Kaycee Kalpin for generously sharing her experience in agile marketing. And to Drew Neisser and Adam Franklin who gave great advice on how to write and publish a book. Thanks to Carey Evans and Matt Pickens for great quotes. We give a big shout-out to the authors of the *Challenger Customer* for their inspiration and to the whole team at ITSMA for the great work that you do. ABM would not be where it is without you.

Our colleagues who gave support and feedback, Bob Blount, Erin Farrell-Talbot, Karen Finn, Hannah Kelley, Justin Metz, Laticia Miller, Bryan Schnepf, Ian Schnepf, Chris Revell, Lisa Laczynski, Lily Mei, and Paul Vandre. And our network who took the time to share feedback on the book: Robert Abrahamson, Jim Brown, Matthew Carollo, Wayne Cerullo, Jenna Chambers, Natalie Cunningham, James Griffin, Patrick Hobson, Erik Johnson, Kate Johnson, Shannon Larkin, Paul Mattioli, Lucy Railton, Jim Rose, Adam Rosenberg, Karsten Russell-Wood, Jon Samsel, and Melinda Stuart. You all helped steer our direction.

Printed in the USA
CPSIA information can be obtained
at www.ICGtesting.com
JSHW011031100424
60923JS00003B/10